CD JACKET COLLECTION

P·I·E BOOKS

MUSIGRAPHICS 1
—A Collection of LP and CD Art—

Copyright © 1991 P·I·E BOOKS

First Edition December 1991

ISBN4-938586-26-6 C3070

P·I·E BOOKS
#407, 4-14-6, Komagome, Toshima-ku, Tokyo 170, JAPAN
Phone 03-3949-5010 Fax 03-3949-5650

CONTENTS

ACKNOWLEDGEMENT

この場を借りて以下の人達に心から感謝致します。
彼達の協力がなければ本書は実現しなかったでしょう。また、彼達に手伝ってもらった結果を、
彼達自身に見ていただける段階までたどり着けたことを嬉しく思います。

貴重な資料を提供してくれたジムコレコードの永井研氏、米沢憲一氏、
えとせとらレコードの遠藤哲夫氏、WAVE六本木店の望月俊彦氏。
作品選びの場を提供してくれたHMV渋谷の平岩孝氏、笹崎利幸氏、川瀧義彦氏、
芽瑠璃堂渋谷店の前店長の中山義雄氏、山野楽器。
作品を提供してくれた石岡瑛子デザイン室、ノーマン　ムーア、トミー　スティール、
ジェリー　ヘイデン、ジェーン　ボガード、チャック　ベンソン、ケビン　ホスマン、
メラニー　ベニー、デビー　サイモン、トニー　ウィルソン、ケビン　レーガン。
快く掲載を許可してくれたバン　オリバー、ポール　ホワイト。
貴重なアドバイスをしてくれたジュンコ　ウォングさん。
撮影で協力してくれたフォトスタジオテクネの佐藤尚一氏。
編集上の貴重なアドバイスをしてくれたエリック　シャリーン、パメラ　バジリオ。
真夜中の国際電話に付き合ってくれた加藤格さんとダグラス　アルソップ、
通訳をしてくれた山尾ゆりさん。
アシスタントフォトグラファーの宮本億三さんと岡本貴之さん。
撮影の準備、原稿の整理を手伝ってくれた佐久間尚美さんと門馬由美さん。

本書にジャケットを掲載した、以下のレコード会社にも感謝したい。

JAPAN
アルファ、アメリカーナ、エイベックストラックス、バンダイ、BMGビクター、
キャプテン、センチュリー、日本コロムビア、クラウン、D.I.W、江戸屋、エピックソニー、
エクスプロージョンワークス、ファイル、フォーライフ、ファンハウス、ハミングバード、
インナーディレクツ、J.A.P、ジムコ、キング、キティ、ロブ、MCAビクター、メルダック、
ミディ、MMG、MSI、NECアベニュー、日本フォノグラム、P-VINE、ポリドール、
ポリスター、ポニーキャニオン、パスリン、クアトロ（パルコ）、SFC音楽出版、創美企画、
ソニー、スパイラル、テイチク、徳間ジャパン、東芝EMI、トランジスター、バップ、
ビクター音産、ビニールジャパン、ヴァージンジャパン、ヴィヴィットサウンド、
ワーナーパイオニア、WAVE、WEAミュージック。
OVERSEAS
4AD、A&M、エース、アシッドジャズ、アラビアンカ、アリゲイター、アリスタ、
アトランティック、アタック、バークレイ、BBC、ベアーファミリー、ベガーズバンケット、
ブルームーン、ブルーノート、BMG、ブッダミュージック、キャピトル、
チャンピオン、カリスマ、クリサリス、シティービート、クレイ、コックトー、クリエイション、CTI、
デリシャスビニール、ECM、エレクトラ　アサイラム　ノンサッチ、EMI、エマーシー、
エニグマ、エンシン、ファクトリー、FFRR、ファイアー、ゲフィン、ゴールドキャッスル、
グラマヴィジョン、グリーンスリーブス、I.R.S、イマジナリーエンターテイメント、
アイランド、ジャロ、カズ、キッチンウェアー、ライン、ロンドン、ルーク、メニィー、MCA、
マーキュリー、ミュート、ネイティブ、ワンリトルインディアン、アウル、ベイズリーパーク、
フォノグラム、プレイイットアゲインサム、ポリドール、ポップラマ、プリオリティー、
プライベートミュージック、プロファイル、クエスト、RCA、リレイティビィヴィー、
リプライズ、リズムキング、ロジャー&コンティティ、ラフトレード、ラウンダー、
ルーモアー、リコーディスク、S.S.T.、SBK、ミキュウーエル、サヤ、
ソニーミュージックオーストラリア、ソニーミュージックインターナショナル、ソニーミュージックUK、
タモキーワムベジ、テレスター、テノアボッサ、サードマインド、トリプルアース、
トロージャン、ヴァージン、ボイスプリント、ワーナーブラザース、ワーナーミュージックUK、
WEA、ワーカーズプレイタイム、ゼイダ、ZTT。

ジャケットを掲載したにもかかわらず、情報不足でクレジットに名前が載らなかった全てのデザイナー、
イラストレイター、フォトグラファー、その他の人達にも感謝したい。

ピエ・ブックス編集部

We would like to express our heartfelt thanks to the many companies and
individuals without whose help, advice, and
cooperation this book could not have been published:

Ken Nagai and Kenichi Yonezawa of Jimco Records,
Tetsuo Endo of Etcetera Records, Toshihiko Mochizuki of Wave, Roppongi,
and Junko Wong for their advice;
Takashi Hiraiwa, Toshiyuki Sasazaki, Yoshihiko Kawataki of HMV, Shibuya, and
Yoshio Nakayama, former manager of Merurido, Shibuya, and Yamano Music Store
for their assistance in the selection stage;
Eiko Design Inc., Norman Moore, Tommy Steele, Jeri Heiden,
Jane Bogart, Chuck Benson, Kevin Hosmann, Melanie Penny, Debbie Symons,
Tony Wilson, and Keven Reagan for submitting their designs;
Vaughan Oliver and Paul White for allowing us to use their work;
Shoichi Sato of Techne Studio for photography;
Pamela Virgilio and Eric Chaline for their editorial advice;
Itaru Kato and Douglas Allsopp for staying up all night to make
international phone calls; **Yuri Yamao** for interpreting;
Yasuzo Miyamoto and Takayuki Okamoto for assisting the photographer;
Yumi Monma and Naomi Sakuma for photographic styling and helping organize the manuscript.

Our thanks also go to the following companies for submitting sample jackets:

JAPAN

Alfa, Americana, Avextrex, Bandai, BMG Victor, Captain, Century, Columbia. Crown,
D.I.W. Edoya, Epic Sony, Explosion Works, File, For Life, Fun House, Humming Bird,
Inner Directs, J.A.P, Jimco, King, Kitty, Lob, MCA Victor, Meldac, Midy, MMG,
MSI, NEC Avenue, Phonogram, P-vine, Polydor, Polystar, Pony Canyon, Puzzline,
Quattro (Parco), SFC Music Publisher, Sohbi, Sony, Spiral, Teichiku,
Tokuma Japan, Toshiba-EMI, Transistor, Vap, Victor Musical Industries,
Vinyl Japan, Virgin Japan, Vivid Sound, Warner Pioneer, Wave, and Wea Music,
OVERSEAS

4AD, A&M, Ace, Acid Jazz, Ala Bianca, Alligator, Arista, Atlantic, Attack,
Barclay, BBC, Bear Family, Beggars Banquet, Blue Moon, Blue Note, BMG, Buda Music,
Capitol, Champion, Charisma, Chrysalis, City Beat, Clay, Cocteau, Creation, CTI,
Delicious Vinyl, ECM, Elektra Asylum Nonesuch, EMI, Emarcy, Enigma, Ensign,
Factory, FFRR, Fire, Geffen, Gold Castle, Gramavision, Greensleeves,
I.R.S., Imaginary Entertainment, Island, Jaro, Kaz, Kitchenware, Line, London, Luke,
Many, MCA, Mercury, Mute, Native, One Little Indian, Owl,
Paisley Park, Phonogram, Play It Again Sam, Polydor, Popllama, Priority, Private Music, Profile,
Qwest, RCA, Relativity, Reprise, Rhythm King, Rodgers & Comtiti, Rough Trade, Rounder, Rumour, Rykodisk,
S.S.T., SBK, Sequel, Sire, Sony Music Australia, Sony Music International, Sony Music UK,
Tamoki-Wambesi, Telstar, Tenor Vossa, Third Mind, Triple Earth, Trojan,
Virgin, Voice Print, Warner Bros, Warner Music UK, WEA, Workers Playtime, Zeida, and ZTT.

Finally, we would like to thank the designers, illustrators, and
photographers whose work has been included in this book, but who could
not be credited because of lack of information.

P·I·E BOOKS

いわゆるポップミュージックは消費される事で常に変化し、活発な新陳代謝を繰り返す事でその商品性を保ってきた訳である。そういった性質上、ポップミュージックが時代性を強く反映する側面を持ち合わせた事はいうまでもなく、そこが若い層に支持された一つの要素ではないだろうか。消費という本質を内包することによって時代の気分や雰囲気、躍動感また文化までも巻き込んでしたたかに増殖するポップミュージックは、まさに時代を映す鏡である。

言うまでもなくポップミュージックはその時代その時代の支持層に強い影響を与え、それに触発されて、いくつもの新しい価値観やムーブメントが生まれた。いわゆるサブカルチャーと呼ばれるものの誕生である。

そんなポップミュージックを核とするサブカルチャーの中で重要な位置を占めているのがジャケットデザインではないだろうか。何も時代性を有するのはポップミュージックだけに限らない。ポップミュージック自体を包み込むジャケットデザイン、もしくはそれに関連するアートといった要素も時代性と無関係ではない。むしろ、肝心の音以上に時代性を強力に打ち出している作品も少なくない。ミュージシャンをはじめとするクリエイター達はジャケットデザインを音と同様に一つの自己表現手段と考えトータルアートとしての可能性を模索し始めたのだ。

アートはポップミュージックの持つ時代性と結びつくことによって一般性を獲得し、一方のポップミュージックはアートの持つ芸術性と結びつきその付加価値を高めることに成功した。昔から、ビジュアルと音が密接に関わり合い互いに発展してきた訳で、ポップミュージックという消費性の強い音楽と、消費性という点ではクエスチョンマークが付くアートとのユニークな出会いは、サブカルチャーを代表するような優れた作品を数多く生んだ。

現在もポップミュージックは依然として消費という本質を内包しつつその表情を微妙に変化させている。一方のジャケットデザインは今、避けて通ることのできない転機を迎えた。80年代後半から急激にその加速度を増したCD化の波である。現在、日本国内においてはその市場のほぼ9割を占めるに至る状況である。日本国内ではLP盤はごく一部の特殊な例を除いてもはや存在しなくなったといっても過言ではないだろう。1991年は日本において音の面でのLPからCDへの移行がほぼ完全な形で終了した年である。海外では日本ほどの極端なCD化は見られなかったものの、ここ数年の間に確実に状況は進行するだろう。

LPからCDへの移行はあくまで中身の音をCD化させただけであって、デザイン上のスムーズな移行を実現するといった配慮が全くなされなかったように思う。その結果、ジャケットデザインの対応の遅ればかりが目立つ作品が店頭にならぶようになった。例を上げると、かつてはジャケットアートの名盤と評価された作品もそのまま無造作にCDサイズに縮小されただけである。かつてジャケットアートに自分の新しい可能性を見出そうと試みたミュージシャンやクリエイター達はどんな思いを抱いてその作品を眺めたのだろうか。

しかし、ここ1、2年のジャケットデザインの状況を眺めているとやっと一時期の混乱から抜け出した感じがする。例にだしたような安易なCDも徐々にだが数を減らしつつある。やっと音のCD化にデザインのCD化が追いつきつつあるようだ。急激なCD化によるデザイン的には混乱した状況が、LP時代に確立した要素とCD特有の新しい要素を加えアナログからデジタルに再構築されつつある。デザイン分野のCD化が完全に完了したとは言い切れないが、とりあえず今後のジャケットデザインの主流となりうる可能性を秘めたスタイルがほぼ出そろった状況と言えるのではないだろうか。

本書はジャケットデザインのターニングポイントとも言える1990年に企画された。ポップミュージックもしくはジャケットデザインが時代性と切りはなして考えられないように、本書もグラフィック図書の基本的性格は残しつつも時代を若干でも映しだせたら素敵だと考えている。

この本をご覧になる方達が、現在の混沌としつつも新しい可能性を手探りで捜し試行錯誤を繰り返しているようなジャケットデザインを取りまく状況を少しでも感じとっていただければ幸いである。

ピエ・ブックス編集部

Pop music—like other consumer items—is constantly changing. It maintains its popularity by constantly renewing the products on the market. It goes without saying that one of the main reasons why pop music is favored by the young is that it reflects the mood and spirit of the times. Pop music strongly influences its fans, giving rise to new values and movements. In other words, it generates subculture.

Jacket design is an important element of pop subculture. It is not just pop music that reflects the spirit of the times, jacket design, packaging, and jacket art are just as significant. Many jackets convey the mood of a period better than the music itself. Musicians and other artists have started to realize that jacket design is a total art form that has the same potential for self-expression as music.

Art has gained currency by being associated with pop music, and the status of pop music has been enhanced by its association with art. Since ancient times, visual art and music have been closely related and have helped each other develop. The unique connection between pop music, a major consumer item, and art, a minor consumer item, creates subculture.

Jacket design has reached a turning point. CDs have rapidly increased in popularity since the latter half of the eighties. In Japan, CDs now represent ninety percent of the market. It will be difficult for LPs to survive at all, except for some special cases. Nineteen-ninety-one will probably be remembered as the year CDs completely overtook LPs in the Japanese market. Although the growth of CDs in the rest of the world has not been quite as dramatic, there too a similar trend has been apparent in the past several years.

The revolution in sound quality that took place when CDs replaced LPs was not accompanied by a change in jacket design. This lag can be clearly seen in the shops: many CDs use the same designs as the LPs they replace. Masterpieces of jacket art that were once prized are now shot down to CD format.

However, in the past two years, CD Jacket design has shown some signs of improvement. There are fewer inappropriate designs, and we can look forward to a time when the quality of jacket design will finally match sound quality. This is an opportunity to develop a new style that will become the model for the jacket design of the future.

This book was planned in 1990, at the turning point of jacket design, and just like pop music and jacket design, the background of the times is an essential element. We hope that MUSIGRAPHICS conveys current conditions in the world of jacket design and will motivate designers and musicians to experiment with new ideas.

P·I·E BOOKS

EDITORIAL NOTES

RECORD CO, : A _____ /B_____
RECORD NO, : C _____

A：原盤会社 /B：国内のレコード会社
C：国内のCD番号
なお、掲載した作品の中には編集作業の間に
レーベルの移動やレコード会社が変わった物もあります。
また、国内のCD番号がクレジットされている全ての作品が、
国内盤を使用しているとは限りません。
あえて輸入盤を掲載している作品もあります。

A: Original record company /B: Domestic record company
C: Domestic CD number
The record companies and labels of
several featured CDs and LPs
changed during the editing of this book.
Although all CD numbers given in the
credits are domestic, in some cases
we have used imported jacket designs.

MiXED MEDIA

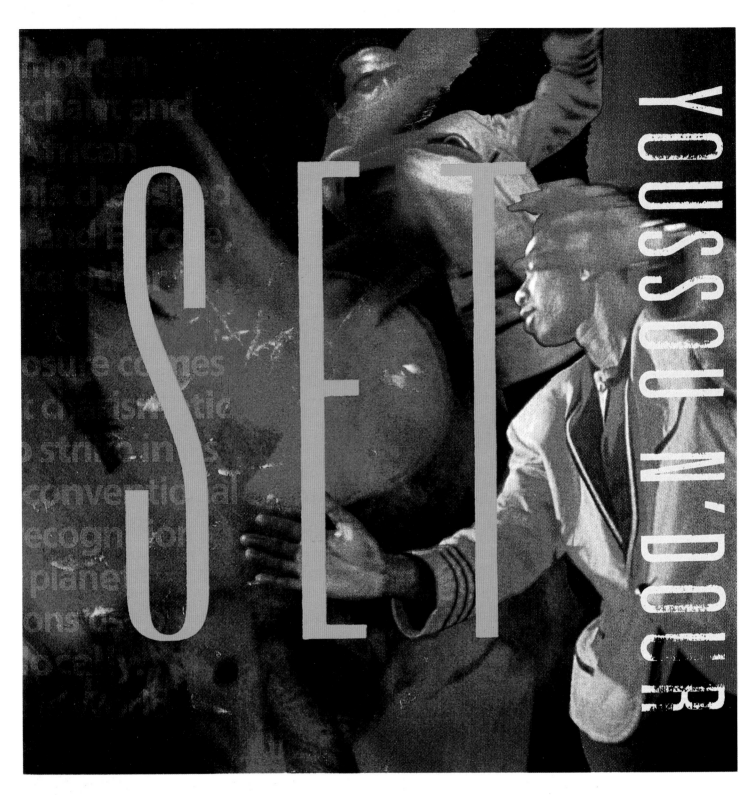

1. YOUSSOU N' DOUR "SET"
DESIGN : RUSSELL MILLS, DAVE COPPENHALL(ME2)
PHOTOGRAPHY : JAK KILBY
YEAR OF RELEASE : 1990
RECORD CO. : VIRGIN/VIRGIN(JAPAN)
RECORD NO. : VJCP-47

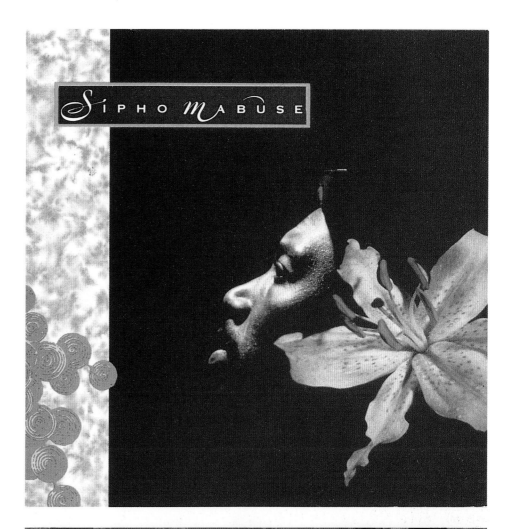

2. SIPHO MABUSE

DESIGN : ICON, LONDON

PHOTOGRAPHY : JEAN-BAPTISTE MONDINO

RECORD CO. : VIRGIN

3. MACEO "FOR ALL THE KING'S MEN"

DESIGN : ALDO SAMPIERI

PHOTOGRAPHY : GEORGE DU BOSE

YEAR OF RELEASE : 1990

RECORD CO. : ISLAND/POLYSTAR(JAPAN)

RECORD NO. : PSCD 1074

4. NEW ORDER "TECHNIQUE"

ART DIRECTION : PETER SAVILLE

DESIGN : PETER SAVILLE ASSOCIATES

YEAR OF RELEASE : 1989

RECORD CO. : FACTORY/COLUMBIA(JAPAN)

RECORD NO. : 25CY-3083

5. LUSH "GALA"

DESIGN : VAUGHAN OLIVER, CHRIS BIGG AT V23

PHOTOGRAPHY : JIM FRIEDMAN

YEAR OF RELEASE : 1990

RECORD CO. : 4AD/COLUMBIA(JAPAN)

RECORD NO. : COCY 6925

6. NEW ORDER "FINE TINE"
ART DIRECTION : PETER SAVILLE
DESIGN : PETER SAVILLE ASSOCIATES
PHOTOGRAPHY : TREVOR KEY
ILLUSTRATION : RICHARD BERNSTEIN
(AFTER A PAINTING)
YEAR OF RELEASE : 1988
RECORD CO. : FACTORY/COLUMBIA(JAPAN)
RECORD NO. : 15CY-5022

7. HAPPY MONDAYS
"PILLSN THRILLS AND BELLYACHES"
ART DIRECTION : CENTRAL STATION DESIGN
DESIGN : CENTRAL STATION DESIGN
ILLUSTRATION : CENTRAL STATION DESIGN
YEAR OF RELEASE : 1990
RECORD CO. : FACTORY/POLYDOR(JAPAN)
RECORD NO. : POCD-1035

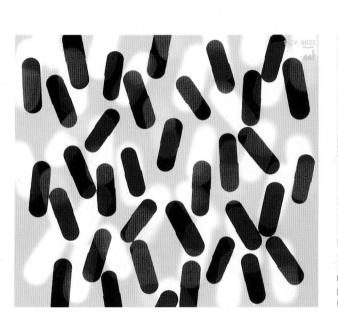

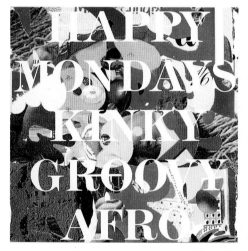

12" Single

8. HAPPY MONDAYS "KINKY GROOVY AFRO"
ART DIRECTION : CENTRAL STATION DESIGN
DESIGN : CENTRAL STATION DESIGN
ILLUSTRATION : CENTRAL STATION DESIGN
YEAR OF RELEASE : 1990
RECORD CO. : FACTORY/POLYDOR(JAPAN)
RECORD NO. : POCD-1034

9. HOUSE OF LOVE "BEATLES AND THE STONES"
DESIGN : DAVID CROW
GRAPHIC PAINTBOX : RICHARD BAKER
PHOTOGRAPHY : PAUL COX
YEAR OF RELEASE : 1990
RECORD CO. : PHONOGRAM

10. RED LORRY YELLOW LORRY "BLOW"
DESIGN : STIFF WEAPON
ILLUSTRATION : LOU
YEAR OF RELEASE : 1989
RECORD CO. : BEGGARS BANQUET/ALFA(JAPAN)
RECORD NO. : ALCB-26

11. KONDO · IMA "TOKYO ROSE"
ART DIRECTION : NORIHIRO HIRAYAMA
DESIGN : HIROAKI SHIMBO
PHOTOGRAPHY : SHIN WATANABE, SYUNDO URAGUCHI
YEAR OF RELEASE : 1990
RECORD CO. : ALFA(JAPAN)
RECORD NO. : ALCA-3

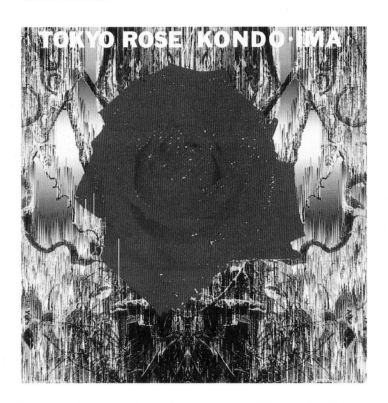

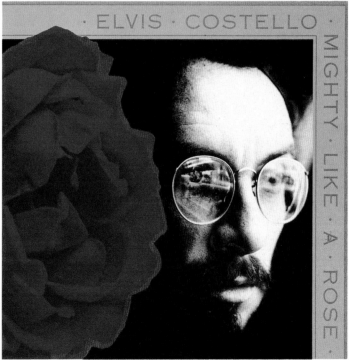

12. ELVIS COSTELLO "MIGHTY LIKE A ROSE"
DESIGN : MIKE KRAGE AND EAMMON SINGER
PHOTOGRAPHY AND HANDTINTING : AMELIA STEIN
YEAR OF RELEASE : 1991
RECORD CO. : WARNER/WARNER PIONEER(JAPAN)
RECORD NO. : WPCP-4344

13. FLESH FOR LULU "PLASTIC FANTASTIC"

ART DIRECTION : STIFF WEAPON

DESIGN : STIFF WEAPON

PHOTOGRAPHY : PAUL COX

YEAR OF RELEASE : 1989

RECORD CO. : BEGGARS BANQUET/ALFA(JAPAN)

RECORD NO. : ALCB-15

14. NEW ORDER "POWER, CORRUPTION & LES"

ART DIRECTION : PETER SAVILLE

DESIGN : PETER SAVILLE ASSOCIATES

ILLUSTRATION : ROSES : FANTIN LATOUR-REPRODUCED

COURTESY OF THE TRUSTEES THE NATIONAL GALLERY LONDON

YEAR OF RELEASE : 1983

RECORD CO. : FACTORY/COLUMBIA(JAPAN)

RECORD NO. : 25CY-3109

15. ANASTASIA SCREAMED
"LAUGHING DOWN THE LIMEHOUSE"

ART DIRECTION : JOE MONTGOMERY

DESIGN : JOE MONTGOMERY

YEAR OF RELEASE : 1990

RECORD CO. : FIRE

16. GONTITI "DEVONIAN BOYS"
ART DIRECTION : MICK ITAYA
PHOTOGRAPHY : TAKATOSHI SHIMIZU
YEAR OF RELEASE : 1990
RECORD CO. : EPIC SONY(JAPAN)
RECORD NO. : ESCB-1050

17. WORKSHY "THE GOLDEN MILE"
DESIGN : TONY McDERMOTT
PHOTOGRAPHY : PETE MOSS
YEAR OF RELEASE : 1989
RECORD CO. : MAGNET/VICTOR
RECORD NO. : VDP-1509

20. NOBODY'S CHILD "ROMANIAN ANGEL APPEAL"
DESIGN : WHEREFORE ART
PHOTOGRAPHY : NOBBY CLARK
MONTAGE : DAVID PALMER
YEAR OF RELEASE : 1990
RECORD CO. : WARNER/WARNER PIONEER(JAPAN)
RECORD NO. : WPCP-3639

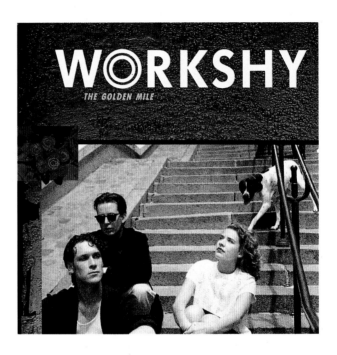

18. MOUTH MUSIC
DESIGN : BRIDGES & WOODS
PHOTOGRAPHY : GAVIN EVANS
YEAR OF RELEASE : 1990
RECORD CO. : TRIPLE EARTH MUSIC
/CBS SONY(JAPAN)
RECORD NO. : CSCS-5314

**19.SONS OF THE DESERT
"THE ELEPHANT SESSIONS"**
ART DIRECTION : SIMON RYAN
DESIGN : SIMON RYAN
PHOTOGRAPHY : ANDY CATLIN
ILLUSTRATION : SIMON RYAN
YEAR OF RELEASE : 1990
RECORD CO. : QUATTRO(JAPAN)
RECORD NO. : QTCY-2002

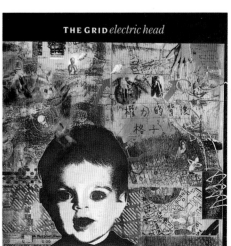

21. DAEVID ALLEN "THE AUSTRALIAN YEARS"

ART DIRECTION : MARK JENKINS

DESIGN : GIULIA HETHERINGTON

YEAR OF RELEASE : 1991

RECORD CO. : VOICE PRINT

22.THE BEAUTIFUL SOUTH "CHOKE"

DESIGN : RYAN ART

YEAR OF RELEASE : 1990

RECORD CO. : LONDON/POLYDOR(JAPAN)

RECORD NO. : POCD-1037

23. THE GRID "ELECTRIC HEAD"

COVER ART : PAUL DAVEIS

DESIGN : STYLOROUGE

YEAR OF RELEASE : 1990

RECORD CO. : WEA/WEA(JAPAN)

RECORD NO. : WMC5-179

Front

24. DAVID BYRNE "REI MOMO"

DESIGN : DOUBLESPACE NY, DAVID BYRNE

PHOTOGRAPHY : KURIGAMI

YEAR OF RELEASE : 1989

RECORD CO. : SIRE/MMG(JAPAN)

RECORD NO. : 25XE-12

Back

25. BUCK-TICK "TABOO"
ART DIRECTION : KEN SAKAGUCHI
PHOTOGRAPHY : KAZUHIRO KITAOKA
YEAR OF RELEASE : 1989
RECORD CO. : VICTOR(JAPAN)
RECORD NO. : VDR-1579

26. TODD RUNDGREN "HEARLY HUMAN"
DESIGN : TODD RUNDGREN
ELECTRIC IMAGE CONPOSITION : TODD & LISA OSTA
YEAR OF RELEASE : 1989
RECORD CO. : WARNER/WARNER PIONEER(JAPAN)
RECORD NO. : 22P2-2719

27. BUCK-TICK "HURRY UP MODE"
ART DIRECTION : KEN SAKAGUCHI
PHOTOGRAPHY : MAMORU TSUKADA
YEAR OF RELEASE : 1990
RECORD CO. : VICTOR(JAPAN)
RECORD NO. : VICL-3

28. KYOSUKE HIMURO "NEO FASCIO"

CREATIVE DIRECTION : OSAMU MORIYA(LOUISIANA COMPANY)

ART DIRECTION : OSAMU MORIYA, HIROYOSHI KITAZAWA

DESIGN : HIROYOSHI KITAZAWA, MIYAKO MATSUO

PHOTOGRAPHY : TOSHITAKA NIWA

GRAPHIC PAINT BOX : HIROKI HORIUCHI(KOYO COLOR)

YEAR OF RELEASE : 1989

RECORD CO. : TOSHIBA EMI(JAPAN)

RECORD NO. : CT32-5555

29. DAVID VAN TIEGHEM "STRANGE CARGO"

ART DIRECTION : MARK LARSON

PHOTOGRAPHY : PENNY GENTIEU

ART COORDINATION : TISH FRIED

YEAR OF RELEASE : 1989

RECORD CO. : PRIVATE MUSIC

30. DAVID GRANT "ANXIOUS EDGE"
DESIGN : 3 ST(THIRST)
PHOTOGRAPHY : EDDIE MONSOON
YEAR OF RELEASE : 1990
RECORD CO. : ISLAND/POLYSTAR(JAPAN)
RECORD NO. : PSCD-1076

31. LOU REED "RETRO"
DESIGN : STYLOROUGE
YEAR OF RELEASE : 1989
RECORD CO. : BMG

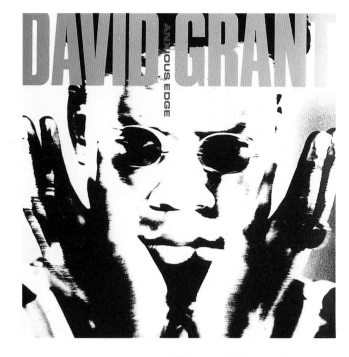

32. JOHN ZORN "FILM WORKS 1986-1990"
DESIGN : ANTHONY LEE, TOMOKO TANAKA
YEAR OF RELEASE : 1990
RECORD CO. : WAVE(JAPAN)
RECORD NO. : EVA 2024

Front

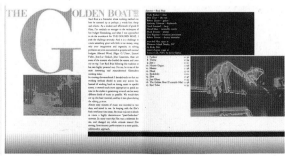

TOCT-5647

33. YUKIHIRO TAKAHASHI
"BROAD CAST FROM HEAVEN"
ART : TADANORI YOKOO
DESIGN : YOSHIKI KANAZAWA
YEAR OF RELEASE : 1990
RECORD CO. : TOSHIBA EMI(JAPAN)
RECORD NO. : TOCT-5647

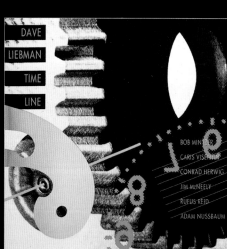

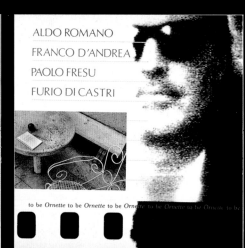

37. THE ART OF NOISE "IN·NO·SENSE? NONSENS!"
ART DIRECTION : JOHN PASCHE
DESIGN : ROLAND WILLIAMS
PHOTOGRAPHY : ALAN DAVID-TU.
YEAR OF RELEASE : 1987
RECORD CO. : CHRYSALIS/TOSHIBA EMI(JAPAN)
RECORD NO. : CP32-5510

38. CAN "RITE TIME"
ART DIRECTION : WERNER O. RICHER
YEAR OF RELEASE : 1990
RECORD CO. : MERCURY/PHONOGRAM(JAPAN)
RECORD NO. : PPD-1131

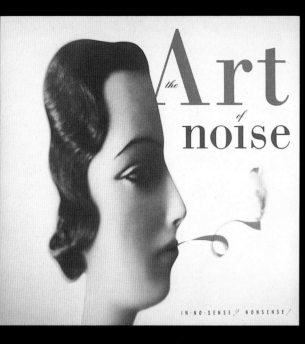

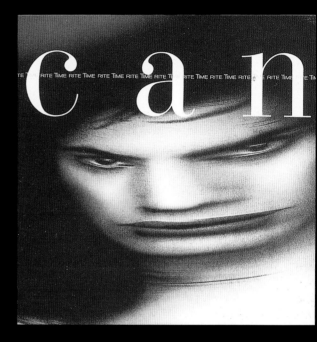

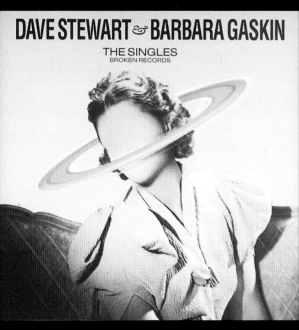

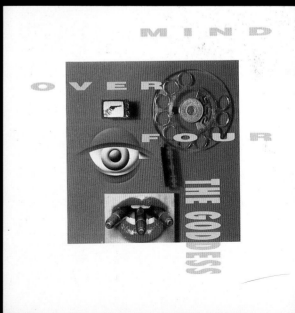

**39. DAVE STEWART AND
BARBARA GASKIN "THE SINGLES"**

40. MIND OVER FOUR "THE GODDES"
YEAR OF RELEASE : 1990

41. NEW DAYS NEWZ "BIG GAME"
ART DIRECTION : HIRONORI KOMIYA
DESIGN : YOKO NAKANO
YEAR OF RELEASE : 1990
RECORD CO. : CBS SNOY(JAPAN)
RECORD NO. : CSCL-1515

42. FLIPPER'S GUITAR "CAMERA TALK"
ART DIRECTION : MITSUO SHINDO
DESIGN : SAWAKO NAKAJIMA
PHOTOGRAPHY : KENJI MIURA
RECORD CO. : POLYSTAR(JAPAN)
RECORD NO. : PSCR-1008

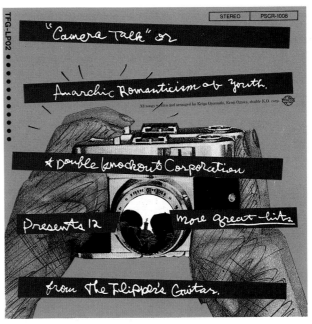

43. GRASS VALLEY "STYLE"
ART DIRECTION : YASUTAKA KATO
PHOTOGRAPHY : KOH HOSOKAWA
YEAR OF RELEASE : 1988
RECORD CO. : CBS SONY(JAPAN)
RECORD NO. : 32DH-5080

44. THE TIME "PANDEMONIUM"
ART DIRECTION : DEBORAH NORCROSS,
JANET LEVINSON
DESIGN : DEBORAH NORCROSS
YEAR OF RELEASE : 1990
RECORD CO. : REPRISE/WARNER PIONEER(JAPAN)
RECORD NO. : WPCP-3641

45. HIROSHIMA "EAST"
ART DIRECTION : NANCY DONALD,
DAVID COLEMAN
DESIGN : NANCY DONALD, DAVID COLEMAN
PHOTOGRAPHY : STEVE SAKAI
YEAR OF RELEASE : 1989
RECORD CO. : EPIC/EPIC SONY(JAPAN)
RECORD NO. : 25・8P-5219

46. YOSHITAKA MINAMI ¨DAILY NEWS¨
DESIGN : YASUTAKA KATO
PHOTOGRAPHY : KOH HOSOKAWA
ILLUSTRATION : AKIRA YAMAGUCHI
YEAR OF RELEASE : 1988
RECORD CO. : CBS SONY(JAPAN)
RECORD NO. : 32DH-5127

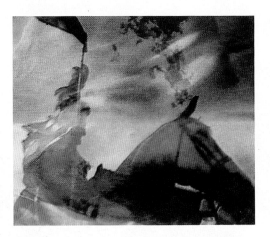

47. BILL NELSON "MAP OF DREAMS"
RECORD CO. : COCTEAU

48. THE TIMES "E FOR EDWARD"
YEAR OF RELEASE : 1989
RECORD CO. : CREATION/VICTOR(JAPAN)
RECORD NO. : VICP-37

49. "PRIVATE MUSIC SAMPLER 5"
ART DIRECTION : NORMAN MOORE
DESIGN : NORMAN MOORE
YEAR OF RELEASE : 1990
RECORD CO. : PRIVATE MUSIC

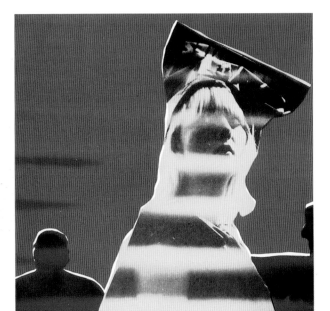

50. JERRY GARCIA "THE WHEEL"
DESIGN : BOB SEIDEMANN
PHOTOGRAPHY : BOB SEIDEMANN
RECORD CO. : GRATEFUL DEAD PRODUCTION
/MSI(JAPAN)
RECORD NO. : GDCD-900656

51. TANGERINE DREAM "LILY ON THE BEACH"
ART DIRECTION : NORMA MOORE
DESIGN : NORMAN MOORE
PHOTO ART DIRECTION : HEIDI BAUMGARTEN
PHOTOGRAPHY : IAN LOGAN
PHOTO CONCEPT : MONICA FROESE
YEAR OF RELEASE : 1989
RECORD CO. : PRIVATE MUSIC /BMG VICTOR(JAPAN)
RECORD NO. : R32P-1250

**52. P.J.B. FEATURING HANNAH AND HER SISTERS
"BRIDGE OVER TROUBLED WATER"**
ART DIRECTION : KLAUS PELZER
YEAR OF RELEASE : 1991
RECORD CO. : CBS

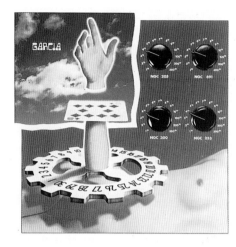  

12″ Single

53. BIG DIPPER "SLAM"
DESIGN : DOUBLE SPACE
PHOTOGRAPHY : MITCHELL KEARNEY
YEAR OF RELEASE : 1990
RECORD CO. : EPIC

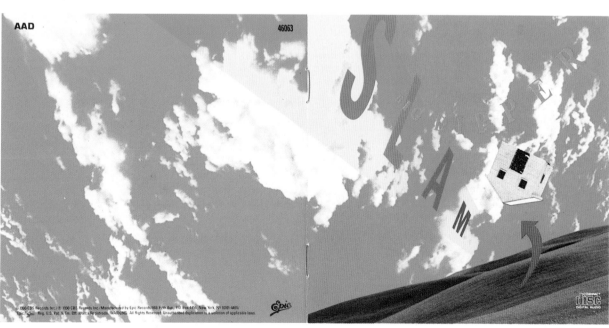

Back & Front

54. ABDEL GADIR SALIM
"NUJUM AL-LAIL-STARS OF THE NIGHT"
DESIGN : DAVID FARROW
PHOTOGRAPHY : JAK KILBY
YEAR OF RELEASE : 1989
RECORD CO. : ACE/KING(JAPAN)
RECORD NO. : KICP 2042

55. PEREGOYO Y SU COMBO VACANA
"TROPICALISIMO"
ART DIRECTION : MICHAEL COVEN
DESIGN : IMPETUS
YEAR OF RELEASE : 1989
RECORD CO. : WORLD CIRCUIT

56. CELIA CRUZ "CANTA CELIA CRUZ"
RECORD CO. : PALLADIUM

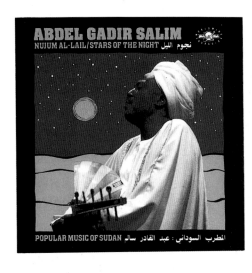

57. WORLD PARTY "WAY DOWN NOW"
YEAR OF RELEASE : 1990
RECORD CO. : ENSIGN

58. PAT METHENY WITH
DAVE HOLLAND & ROY HAYNES
"QUESTION AND ANSWER"
ART DIRECTION : SHED
DESIGN : SHED
PHOTOGRAPHY : CHRISTOPHER KEHOE
YEAR OF RELEASE : 1990
RECORD CO. : GEFFEN

12" Single

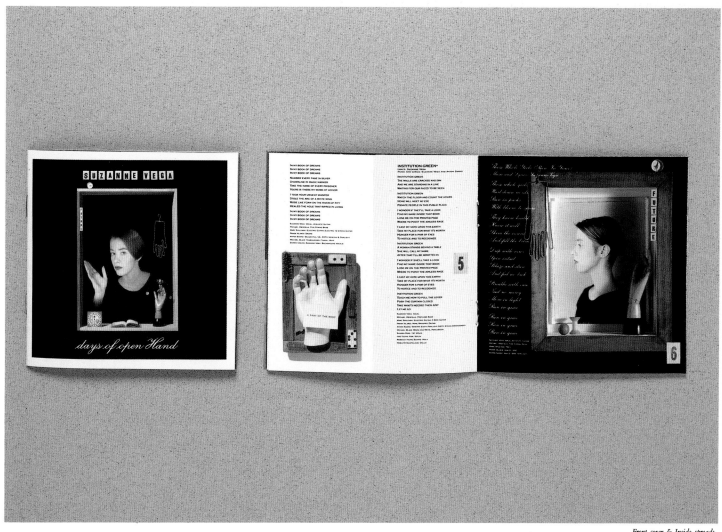

Front cover & Inside spreads

59. SUZANNE VEGA "DAYS OF OPEN HAND"

ART DIRECTION : JEFFREY GOLD, LEN PELTIER
DESIGN : LEN PELTIER
PHOTOGRAPHY : GEOF KERN, GEORGE HOLZ
YEAR OF RELEASE : 1990
RECORD CO. : A & M/PONY CANYON(JAPAN)
RECORD NO. : PCCY-10102

60. SUZANNE VEGA
   "TIRED OF SLEEPING "

YEAR OF RELEASE : 1990
RECORD CO. : A & M

61. MC TUNES "THE NORTH AT ITS HEIGHTS"
ART DRECTION : TREVOR JACKSON
DESIGN : TREVOR JACKSON
PHOTOGRAPHY : ROBERT GOLDSTEIN
YEAR OF RELEASE : 1990
RECORD CO. : ZTT/WEA(JAPAN)
RECORD NO. : WMC5-178

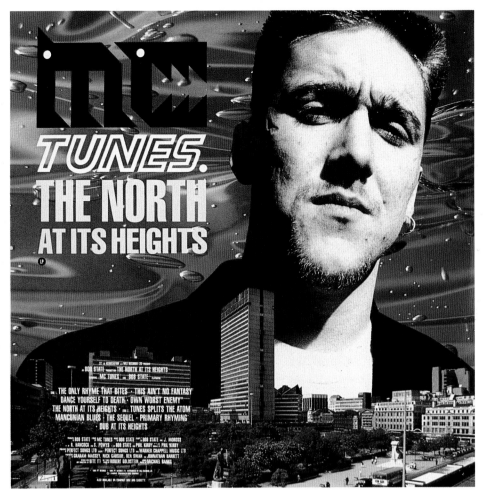

CD Single

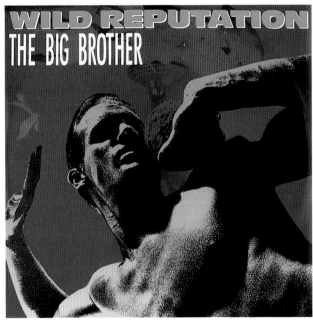

12" Single

62. HOLLY JOHNSON "WHERE HAS LOVE GONE?"
DESIGN : ME COMPANY
PHOTOGRAPHY : RICHARD HOUGHTON
YEAR OF RELEASE : 1990
RECORD CO. : MCA

63. THE BIG BROTHER "WILD REPUTATION"
ART DIRECTION : ART & WORK-MILAN
DESIGN : SERGIO NIGRO
ILLUSTRATION : SERGIO NIGRO
YEAR OF RELEASE : 1990
RECORD CO. : RODGERS AND CONTINI
/AVEX TRAX(JAPAN)

64. NAPALM DEATH "HARMONY CORRUPTION"
ART DIRECTION : DAVID WINDMILL
PHOTOGRAPHY : TIM HUBBARD
YEAR OF RELEASE : 1990
RECORD CO. : EARACHE/VAP
RECORD NO. : 85053

65. KILLING JOKE "AMERICA"
DESIGN : BILL SMITH STUDIO
ILLUSTRATION : ANDRZEJ KLIMOWSKI
YEAR OF RELEASE : 1988
RECORD CO. : VIRGIN

12" Single

12" Single

66. MARCO POLO FEATURING CHRISTINA ONG
   "THE CALLING "
DESIGN : PAULINE AND TIM EVILL
RECORD CO. : MANY

67. POWER OF DREAMS
   "AMERICAN DREAM"
DESIGN : FLAT EARTH
YEAR OF RELEASE 1991
RECORD CO. : POLYDOR

68. WENDY & LISA "EROICA"
ART DIRECTION : MELANIE NISSEN
DESIGN : INGE SCHAAP
PHOTOGRAPHY : ENRIQUE BADULESCU
YEAR OF RELEASE : 1990
RECORD CO. : VIRGIN/VIRGIN(JAPAN)
RECORD NO. : VJCP-41

69. NAYOBE "PROMISE ME"
DESIGN : TRACY VEAL
PHOTOGRAPHY : JIM CANLFIELD
YEAR OF RELEASE : 1990
RECORD CO. : CBS/EPIC SONY(JAPAN)
RECORD NO. : ESCA-5175

70. MARCHOSAS VAMP "IN KAZMIDITY"
ART DIRECTION : HIGASHI ISHIDA
DESIGN : MASAHARU TANAKA, CHITOSE IZUMA
PHOTOGRAPHY : ZIGEN
YEAR OF RELEASE : 1990
RECORD CO. : VICTOR(JAPAN)
RECORD NO. : VICL-66

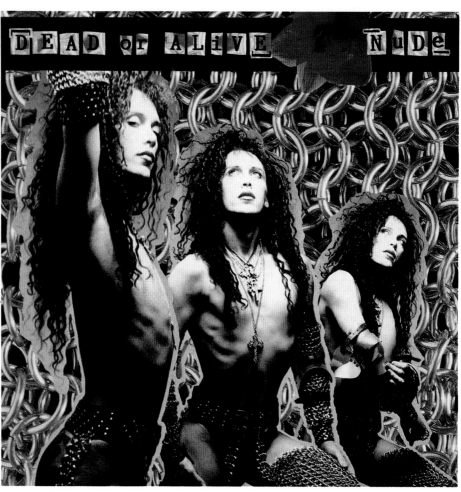

71. INSPIRAL CARPETS "LIFE"
DESIGN : DESIGNLAND
PHOTOGRAPHY : UTE KLAPHAKE
YEAR OF RELEASE : 1990
RECORD CO. : MUTE/ALFA(JAPAN)
RECORD NO. : ALCB-57

72. THE MISSION "CARVED IN SAND"
YEAR OF RELEASE : 1990
RECORD CO. : PHONOGRAM/PHONOGRAM(JAPAN)
RECORD NO. : PPD-1129

73. DEAD OR ALIVE "NUDE"
ART DIRECTION : ANDIE AIRFIX AT SATCRI
DESIGN : ANDIE AIRFIX AT SATCRI
YEAR OF RELEASE : 1988
RECORD CO. : EPIC / EPIC SONY(JAPAN)
RECORD NO. : 25 8P 5160

"OH OH OH GIRLS ARE DANCING"

ART DIRECTION : ART & WORK-MILAN
DESIGN : SERGIO NIGRO
PHOTOGRAPHY : SERGIO NIGRO
ILLUSTRATION : SERGIO NIGRO
YEAR OF RELEASE : 1990
RECORD CO. : RODGERS AND CONTINI
AVEX TRAX(JAPAN)

"TOMORROW NEVER KNOWS"

ART DIRECTION : STYLOROUGE
DESIGN : STYLOROUGE
PHOTOGRAPHY : SIMON FOWLER
YEAR OF RELEASE : 1990
RECORD CO. : SIRE

12" Single

CD Single

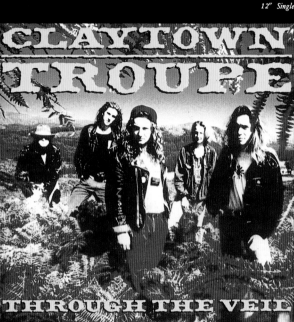

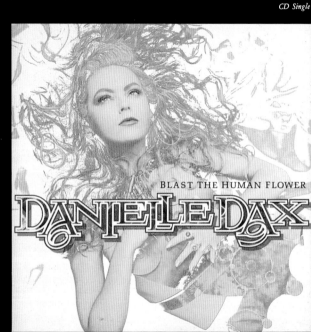

78. HOTHOUSE FLOWERS "GIVE IT UP"
DESIGN : STYLOROUGE
PHOTOGRAPHY : PETER MOUNTAIN
YEAR OF RELEASE : 1990
RECORD CO. : FFRR/POLYDOR(JAPAN)
RECORD NO. : POCD-1009

12" Single

81. PREFAB SPROUT "JORDAN THE EP"
DESIGN : PETER BARRETT, ANDREW BISCOMB
PHOTOGRAPHY : THE DOUGLAS BROTHER
YEAR OF RELEASE : 1990
RECORD CO. : CBS

82. OLETA ADAMS "CIRCLE OF ONE"
DESIGN : THE UNKNOWN PARTNERSHIP
PHOTOGRAPHY : DAVID SCHELNMAN
YEAR OF RELEASE : 1990
RECORD CO. : PHONOGRAM/PHONOGRAM(JAPAN)
RECORD NO. : PHCR-4

83. AREA "AGATE LINES"
CALLIGRAPHY : CHRIS BIGG
PHOTOGRAPHY : BEVERLEY CARRUTHERS
YEAR OF RELEASE : 1990
RECORD CO. : THIRD MIND

84. UCHOTEN "GAN"
ART DIRECTION : YUJI MATSUNOBE,
YOSHINORI MORIKAWA
DESIGN : YUJI MATSUNOBE,
YOSHINORI MORIKAWA
PHOTOGRAPHY : AKIHIKO TSUCHIDA
ILLUSTRATION : KERA
YEAR OF RELEASE : 1988
RECORD CO. : CAPTAIN(JAPAN)
RECORD NO. : CAP-1005-CD

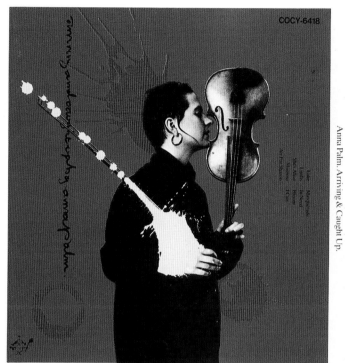

85. ELIZABETH CAUMONT "ACTE 2"
PHOTOGRAPHY : D.RETHALLER
YEAR OF RELEASE : 1990
RECORD CO. : SEVENSEAS/KING(JAPAN)
RECORD NO. : KICP 15

86. ANNA PALM "ARRIVING AND CAUGHT UP"
DESIGN : ME COMPANY
PHOTOGRAPHY : EMILY ANDERSEN
YEAR OF RELEASE : 1990
RECORD CO. : ONE LITTLE
INDIAN/COLUMBIA(JAPAN)
RECORD NO. : COCY-6418

87. BANANARAMA "REMIX ONLY YOUR LOVE"
DESIGN : ANDREW BISCOMB, PETER BARRETT
YEAR OF RELEASE : 1990
RECORD CO. : FFRR

12" Single

88. CABARET VOLTAIRE "RED MECCA"

DESIGN : NEVILLE BRODY, CABARET VOLTAIRE

YEAR OF RELEASE : 1981

RECORD CO. : MUTE

**89. THE ICICLE WORKS
"PERMANENT DAMAGE"**

ART WORK : JONNY MENDELSSON

YEAR OF RELEASE : 1990

RECORD CO. : CBS/EPIC SONY(JAPAN)

RECORD NO. : ESCA-5138

**90. THE JESUS AND MARY CHAIN
"DARKLANDS"**

DESIGN : HELEN BACKHOUSE

PHOTOGRAPHY : TIM BROAD AND JOHN MAYBURY

YEAR OF RELEASE : 1987

RECORD CO. : WEA/WEA(JAPAN)

RECORD NO. : WMC5-205

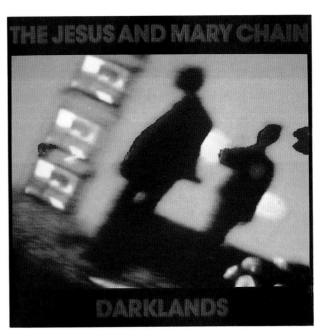

91. JAGATARA "JA·BOM·BE"
DESIGN : YASUO YAGI
PHOTOGRAPHY : YASUO YAGI
YEAR OF RELEASE : 1990
RECORD CO. : CAPTAIN(JAPAN)
RECORD NO. : CAP-1044

92. MOON RIDERS "ISTANBUL MAMBO"
DESIGN : Y.OKUMURA
PHOTOGRAPHY : YOSHIO OTSUKA
YEAR OF RELEASE : 1988
RECORD CO. : CROWN(JAPAN)
RECORD NO. : CRCP-28015

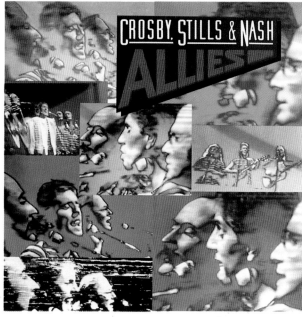

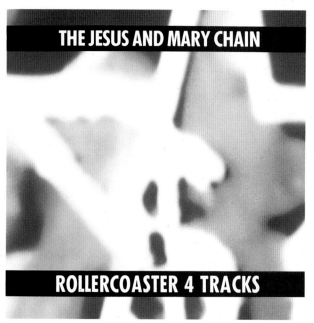

93. CROSBY, STILLS & NASH "ALLIES"
ART DIRECTION : JIMMY WACHTEL, DAWN PATROL
DESIGN : JIMMY WACHTEL, DAWN PATROL
PHOTOGRAPHY : DAVID PETERS
RECORD CO. : ATLANTIC/MMG(JAPAN)
RECORD NO. : AMCY-135

94. THE JESUS AND MARY CHAIN
  "ROLLERCOASTER 4 TRACKS"
YEAR OF RELEASE : 1990
RECORD CO. : WEA/WEA(JAPAN)
RECORD NO. : WMC5-203

95. THE CHECKERS "OOPS!"
ART DIRECTION : AKIRA KAWASHIMA
DESIGN : NORIHIKO UCHIYAMA
PHOTOGRAPHY : KOHKI TAKANO,
SHINSUKE KITA(SASHU)
YEAR OF RELEASE : 1990
RECORD CO. : PONY CANYON(JAPAN)
RECORD NO. : PCCA-00094

96. LIVING COLOUR "VIVID"
ART DIRECTION : STEVE BYRAM
PHOTOGRAPHY : DREW CAROLAN
ILLUSTRATION : THUNDERJOCKEYS
YEAR OF RELEASE : 1988
RECORD CO. : EPIC/EPIC SONY(JAPAN)
RECORD NO. : 25·8P-5048

97. LIVING COLOUR "TIMES UP"
ART DIRECTION : THUNDERJOCKEYS, BYRAM
DESIGN : THUNDERJOCKEYS, BYRAM
PHOTOGRAPHY : LEX VAN PIETER
YEAR OF RELEASE : 1990
RECORD CO. : EPIC/EPIC SONY(JAPAN)
RECORD NO. : ES·CA-5167

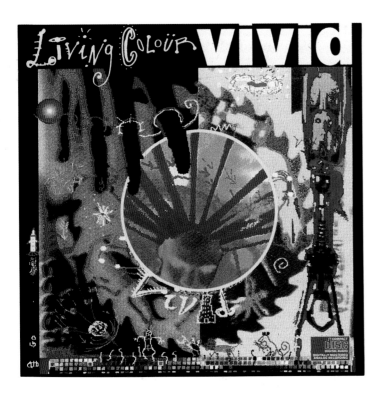

98. P I L "9"
ART DIRECTION : MELANIE NISSAN
DESIGN : MICK HAGGERTY
PHOTOGRAPHY : ROSS HALFIN
COMPUTER MANIPULATION : JAMES FAULKNER
YEAR OF RELEASE : 1990
RECORD CO. : VIRGIN/VIRGIN(JAPAN)
RECORD NO. : VJD-32209

99. SODOM "KING OV HOUSE"
DESIGN : M. OKA
PHOTOGRAPHY : MACOTO MYOUGA
RECORD CO. : CAPTAIN(JAPAN)
RECORD NO. : GONG-6001

Front & Inside spreads

THE CHRISTIANS

COLOUR

100. MAHLATHINI AND MAHOTELLA QUEENS
   "PARIS-SOWETO"
COVER ART : TAKAYUKI TERAKADO
DESIGN : NANA SHIOMI
YEAR OF RELEASE : 1991
RECORD CO. : QUATTRO(JAPAN)
RECORD NO. : QTD-1002

101. THE CHRISTIANS "COLOUR"
YEAR OF RELEASE : 1990
RECORD CO. : ISLAND/POLYSTAR(JAPAN)
RECORD NO. : PSCD-1007

102. HAJIME TACHIBANA
   "BEAUTY AND HAPPY"
ART DIRECTION : HAJIME TACHIBANA
DESIGN : THE STUDIO
PHOTOGRAPHY : KAORU IJIMA
YEAR OF RELEASE : 1987
RECORD CO. : MIDI(JAPAN)
RECORD NO. : MDC7-1027

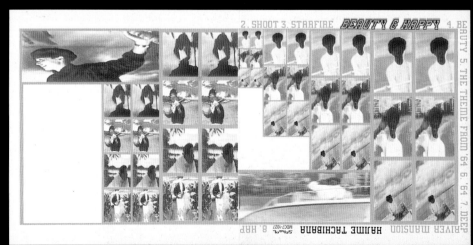

Back & Front

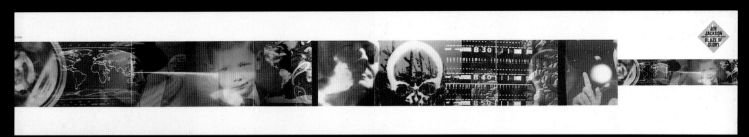

Front & Inside spreads

103. JOE JACKSON "BLAZE OF GLORY"
ART DIRECTION : FRANK OLINSKY, PAT GORMAN,
RICHARD FRANKEL, JOE JACKSON
DESIGN : MANHATTAN DESIGN
PHOTOGRAPHY : SANDRA HABER
YEAR OF RELEASE : 1989
RECORD CO. : A & M/PONY CANYON(JAPAN)
RECORD NO. : D22Y-3363

104. SUSUMU HIRASAWA "JIKU NO MIZU"
ART DIRECTION : KIYOSHI INAGAKI
PHOTOGRAPHY : MADO AND VINCENT
YEAR OF RELEASE : 1989
RECORD CO. : POLYDOR(JAPAN)
RECORD NO. : HOOP 20343

105. SUSUMU HIRASAWA "GOST OF SCIENCE"
ART DIRECTION : KIYOSHI INAGAKI
PHOTOGRAPHY : YOSUKE KOMATSU, NAOKI WADA
YEAR OF RELEASE : 1990
RECORD CO. : POLYDOR(JAPAN)
RECORD NO. : POCH-1009

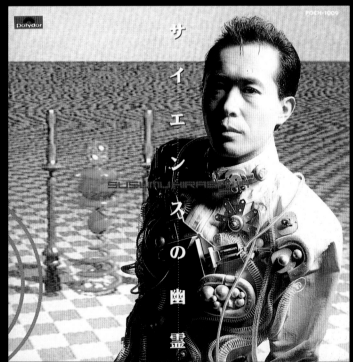

12" Single Front

106. GRACE JONES
"LOVE ON TOP OF LOVE-KILLER KISS"
ART DIRECTION : TOMMY STEELE, JEFFERY FEY
DESIGN : JEFFERY FEY
ILLUSTRATION : RICHARD BERNSTEIN
YEAR OF RELEASE : 1989
RECORD CO. : CAPITOL

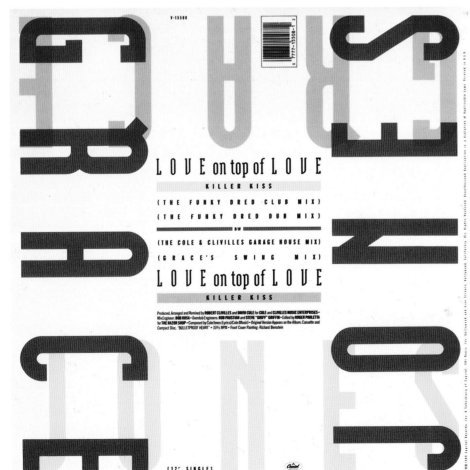

12" Single Back

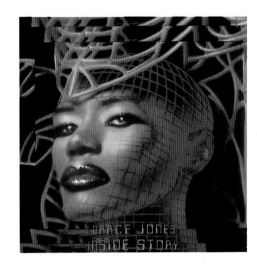

Inside spreads

107. VARIOUS ARTISTS "MEGABASS 2"
SLEEVE : COLLN CHAMBERS
RECORD CO. : TELSTAR

108. GRACE JONES "INSIDE STORY"
ART : RICHARD BERNSTEIN
YEAR OF RELEASE : 1986
RECORD CO. : CAPITOL/TOSHIBA EMI(JAPAN)
RECORD NO. : CP32-5166

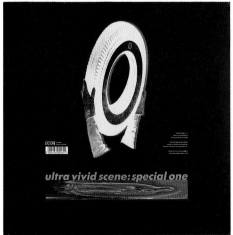

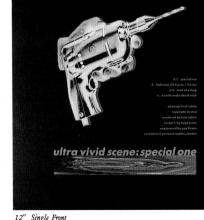

12" Single Back

12" Single Front

109. ULTRA VIVID SCENE "SPECIAL ONE"
DESIGN : VAUGHAN OLIVER/V23.
YEAR OF RELEASE : 1990
RECORD CO. : 4AD

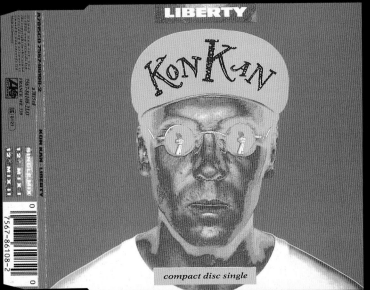

CD Single

110. KON KAN "LIBERTY"

YEAR OF RELEASE : 1990

RECORD CO. : WEA

111. ADRIAN BELEW "MR. MUSIC HEAD"

PHOTOGRAPHY : SANDY OSTROFF

ILLUSTRATION : SANDY OSTROFF

YEAR OF RELEASE : 1989

RECORD CO. : ATLANTIC/MMG(JAPAN)

RECORD NO. : 22P2-2706

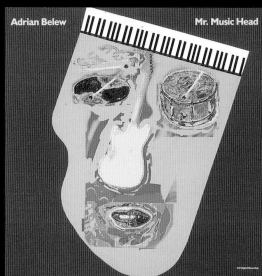

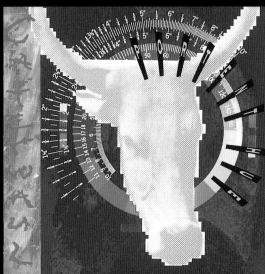

112. CATERWAUL "PORTENT HUE"

ART DIRECTION : FRED DAVIS,

STAN GAMEL WITH CATERWAUL

PHOTOGRAPHY : CLAUDINE

YEAR OF RELEASE : 1990

RECORD CO. : I.R.S./VICTOR(JAPAN)

RECORD NO. : VICP-29

113. MANTRONIX

"DON'T GO MESSIN' WITH MY HEART"

YEAR OF RELEASE : 1991

RECORD CO. : CAPITOL

12" Single

114. JESUS JONES
"INTERNATIONAL BRIGHT YOUNG THING"

DESIGN : STYLOROUGE

PHOTOGRAPHY : SIMON FOWLER

YEAR OF RELEASE : 1991

RECORD CO. : EMI/TOSHIBA EMI(JAPAN)

RECORD NO. : TOCP-6737

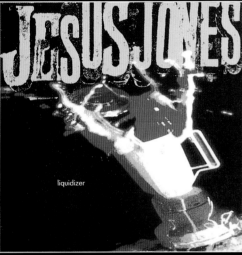

115. JESUS JONES "LIQUIDIZER"

DESIGN : STYLOROUGE

PHOTOGRAPHY : TREVOR ROGERS

YEAR OF RELEASE : 1990

RECORD CO. : EMI/TOSHIBA EMI(JAPAN)

RECORD NO. : TOCP-6106

116. VARIOUS ARTISTS "BEAT THIS!"

DESIGN : GOONER

PHOTOGRAPHY : JURGEN OSTARHILD

YEAR OF RELEASE : 1990

RECORD CO. : RHYTHM KING

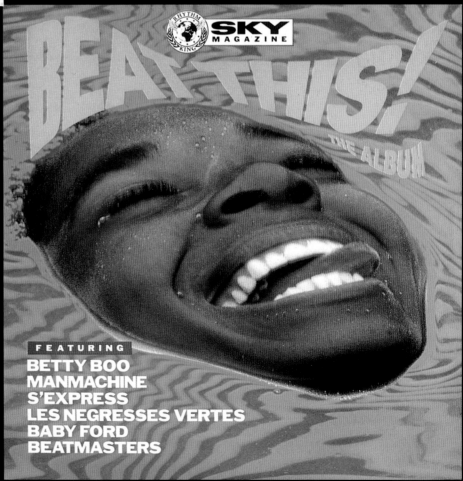

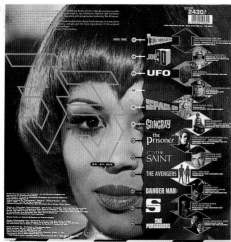

Back

Front

117. F.A.B FEATURING MC PARKER
"POWER THEMES 90"

DESIGN : INTRO.
PHOTOGRAPHY : INTRO.
YEAR OF RELEASE : 1990
RECORD CO. : TELSTAR

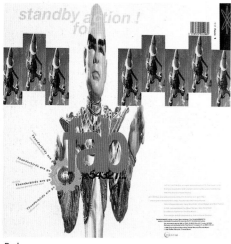

Back

Front

118. F.A.B FEATURING MC PARKER
"THUNDERBIRDS ARE GO!"

DESIGN : INTRONATIONAL RESCUE
PHOTOGRAPHY : INTRONATIONAL RESCUE
YEAR OF RELEASE : 1990
RECORD CO. : TELSTER

PHOTOGRAPHY

119. MADONNA "TRUE BLUE"
ART DIRECTION : JEFFREY KENT AYEROFF, JERI HEIDEN
DESIGN : JERI HEIDEN
PHOTOGRAPHY : HERB RITTS
YEAR OF RELEASE : 1986
RECORD CO. : SIRE/WARNER PIONEER(JAPAN)
RECORD NO. : 18P2-2702

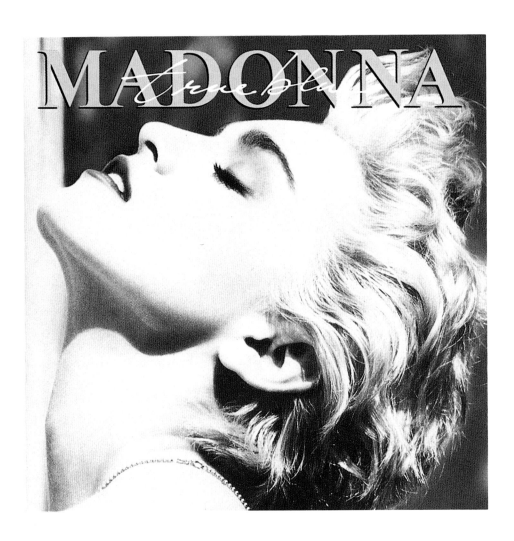

120. STING "THE DREAM OF THE BLUE TURTLES"
ART DIRECTION : MICHAEL ROSS, RICHARD FRANKEL
PHOTOGRAPHY : MAX VADUKUL
YEAR OF RELEASE : 1985
RECORD CO. : A & M/PONY CANYON(JAPAN)
RECORD NO. : D25Y-3276

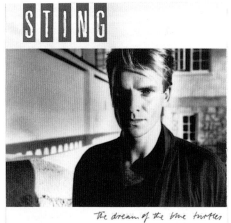

Front & Inside spreads

121. MADONNA "TRUE BLUE"
DESIGN : JERI MCMANUS
PHOTOGRAPHY : HERB RITTS
YEAR OF RELEASE : 1986
RECORD CO. : SIRE

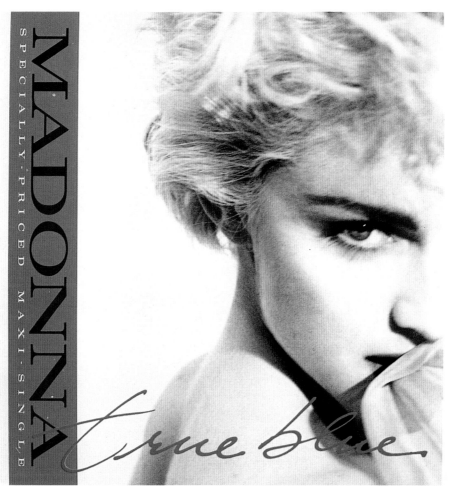

12" Single

22. ROXY MUSIC "HEART STILL BEATING"

ART DIRECTION : STEPHANIE NASH, ANTHONY MICHAEL
DESIGN : STEPHANIE NASH, ANTHONY MICHAEL
PHOTOGRAPHY : TONY MCGEE
YEAR OF RELEASE : 1990
RECORD CO. : VIRGIN/VIRGIN(JAPAN)
RECORD NO. : VJCP-2805

23. PAT BENATAR "TRUE LOVE"

ART DIRECTION : NORMAN MOORE
DESIGN : NORMAN MOORE
PHOTOGRAPHY : RANDEE ST. NICHORAS
YEAR OF RELEASE : 1991
RECORD CO. : CHRYSALIS/TOSHIBA EMI(JAPAN)
RECORD NO. : TOCP-6662

24. VIKTOR LAZLO "CLUB DESERT"

PHOTOGRAPHY : BETTINA RHEIMS
RECORD CO. : POLYDOR/POLYDOR(JAPAN)
RECORD NO. : POOP 20226

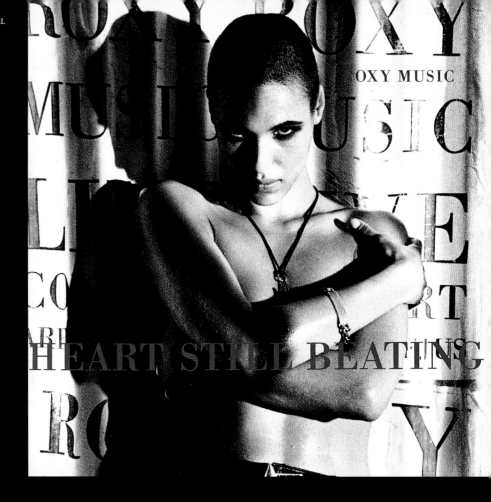

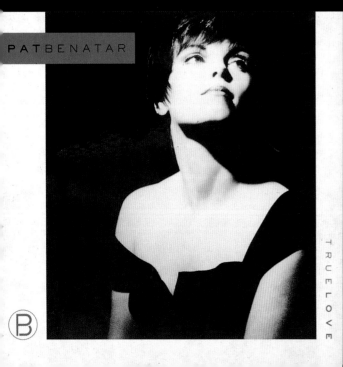

P00P 20226

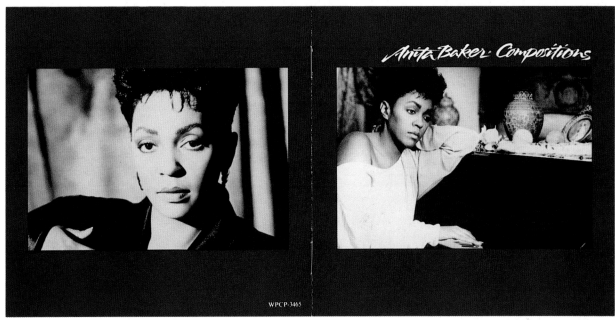

WPCP-3465

Back & Front

125. ANITA BAKER "COMPOSITIONS"
ART DIRECTION : CAROL BOBOLTS, ANITA BAKER
PHOTOGRAPHY : ADRIAN BUCKMASTER
YEAR OF RELEASE : 1990
RECORD CO. : ELEKTRA/WEA(JAPAN)
RECORD NO. : WPCP-3465

126. SADE "DIAMOND LIFE"
DESIGN : GRAHAM SMITH
PHOTOGRAPHY : CHRIS ROBERTS
YEAR OF RELEASE : 1984
RECORD CO. : EPIC/EPIC SONY(JAPAN)
RECORD NO. : 28·8P-5190

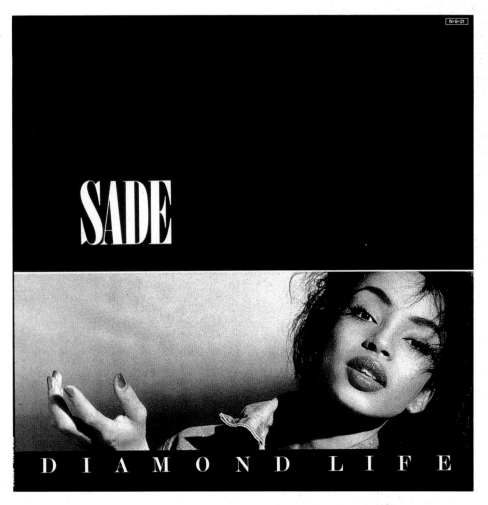

127. SCOTT MERRITT "VIOLET AND BLACK"
ART DIRECTION : DONALD KRIEGER
PHOTOGRAPHY : BOB WITKOWSKI
YEAR OF RELEASE : 1989
RECORD CO. : I.R.S./VICTOR(JAPAN)
RECORD NO. : VICP-30

128. THE BLOW MONKEYS "THIS IS YOUR LIFE"
YEAR OF RELEASE : 1989
RECORD CO. : RCA/BMG VICTOR(JAPAN)
RECORD NO. : B15D-41036

129. ANDY PAWLAK "SHOEBOX FULL OF SECRETS"
DESIGN : MARK WHITEHOUSE
PHOTOGRAPHY : JOSEPH McKENZIE
YEAR OF RELEASE : 1989
RECORD CO. : PHONTANA/PHONOGRAM(JAPAN)
RECORD NO. : PPD-1034

130. REICHI NAKAIDO "E"
ART DIRECTION : PLUS TEN
DESIGN : YOSHIKI KANAZAWA
PHOTOGRAPHY : HISAKO OHKUBO
YEAR OF RELEASE : 1990
RECORD CO. : TOSHIBA EMI(JAPAN)
RECORD NO. : TOCT-5636

131. MASAYUKI YAMAMOTO
   "SAINOU NO HOUKO"
ART DIRECTION : KIYOSHI TAKEHARA
DESIGN : KIYOSHI TAKEHARA
RECORD CO. : HUMMING BIRD(JAPAN)
RECORD NO. : HBCL-7041

132. HIKASU "TEICHOU NA OMOTENASHI"
ART DRECTION : TARO MANABE
DESIGN : YOSHIYUKI SEKI
PHOTOGRAPHY : JUNSUKE TAKIMOTO
RECORD CO. : VAP(JAPAN)
RECORD NO. : VPCC-80429

133. GEORGE MICHAEL
"LISTEN WITHOUT PREJUDICE Vo1"
DESIGN : GEORGE MICHAEL, SIMON HALFON
PHOTOGRAPHY : WEEGEE 1940
YEAR OF RELEASE : 1990
RECORD CO. : EPIC/EPIC SONY(JAPAN)
RECORD NO. : ESCA 5160

COMME des GARCONS
Directed by Seigen Ono

Donald Fagen   The Nightfly

134. REICHI NAKAIDO
"THE NAKAIDO REICHI BOOK"
DESIGN : SHINICHI HARA(RICE CO LTD)
PHOTOGRAPHY : HISAKO OHKUBO
YEAR OF RELEASE : 1988
RECORD CO. : TOSHIBA EMI(JAPAN)
RECORD NO. : CT32-5368

135. COMME DES GARCONS
ART DIRECTION : SEIGEN ONO
YEAR OF RELEASE : 1989
RECORD CO. : TOKUMA(JAPAN)
RECORD NO. : 32JC-408

136. DONALD FAGEN "THE NIGHTFLY"
ART DIRECTION : GEORGE DELMERICO
DESIGN : GEORGE DELMERICO
PHOTOGRAPHY : JAMES HAMILTON
YEAR OF RELEASE : 1982
RECORD CO. : WARNER
/WARNER PIONEER(JAPAN)
RECORD NO. : 20P2-2041

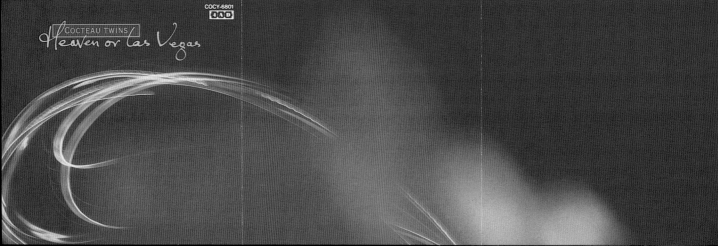

COCY-6801
4AD

COCTEAU TWINS
Heaven or Las Vegas

Front & Inside spreads

138. PAUL McCARTNEY "HIGHLIGHTS!"

ART DIRECTION : PETER SAVILLE
DESIGN : PETER SAVILLE ASSOCIATES
YEAR OF RELEASE : 1990
RECORD CO. : EMI/TOSHIBA EMI(JAPAN)
RECORD NO. : TOCP-6481

Paul McCartney

tripping the live fantastic

highlights!

139. AMBITIOUS LOVERS "GREED"
ART DIRECTION : PAULA ZANES
PHOTOGRAPHY : PAULA ZANES
YEAR OF RELEASE : 1988
RECORD CO. : VIRGIN/VIRGIN(JAPAN)
RECORD NO. : VJD-32085

140. BRYAN FERRY "BÊTE NOIRE"
YEAR OF RELEASE : 1987
RECORD CO. : VIRGIN/VIRGIN(JAPAN)
RECORD NO. : VJD-32002

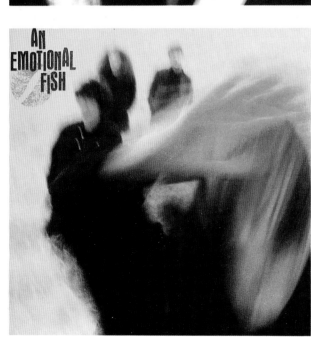 

141. AN EMOTIONAL FISH
DESIGN : STEVE AVERILL
PHOTOGRAPHY : CONOR HORGAN
YEAR OF RELEASE : 1990
RECORD CO. : WEA

142. THE PSYCHEDELIC FURS "BOOK OF DAYS"
DESIGN : RICHARD BUTLER, ALLAN D. MARTIN
PHOTOGRAPHY : PETER ROBATHAN, ALLAN D. MARTIN
YEAR OF RELEASE : 1989
RECORD CO. : CBS/EPIC SONY(JAPAN)
RECORD NO. : ESCA-5074

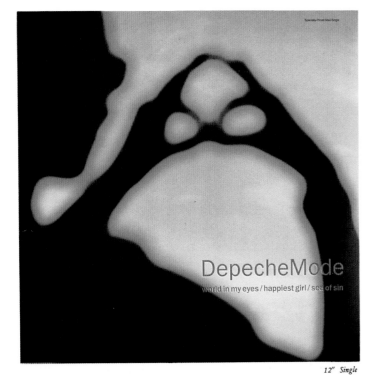

12" Single

12" Single

12" Single Back

12" Single Front

143. DEPECHE MODE "WORLD IN MY EYES"

DESIGN : ANTON CORBIJN, AREA

YEAR OF RELEASE : 1990

RECORD CO. : MUTE

144. DREAM FREQUENCY
"LOVE, PEACE, AND HARMONY"

DESIGN : THE UNKNOWN PARTNERSHIP

PHOTOGRAPHY : ZOE HEALD

YEAR OF RELEASE : 1991

RECORD CO. : CITY BEAT

145. THE ATMOSPHERE INTRODUCING MAE B
"ATM OZ FEAR"

YEAR OF RELEASE : 1990

RECORD CO. : SBK

CD Single

12" Single Back

12" Single Front

146. DEPECHE MODE "POLICY OF TRUTH"

DESIGN : AREA

PHOTOGRAPHY : ANTON CORBIJN

YEAR OF RELEASE : 1990

RECORD CO. : MUTE/ALFA(JAPAN)

RECORD NO. : ALCB-110

147. DEPECHE MODE "POLICY OF TRUTH"

DESIGN : AREA

PHOTOGRAPHY : ANTON CORBIJN

YEAR OF RELEASE : 1990

RECORD CO. : MUTE

CARON WHEELER

DON'T

QUIT

148. CARON WHEELER "DON'T QUIT"
PHOTOGRAPHY : ANDREW MACPHERSON
YEAR OF RELEASE : 1991
RECORD CO. : BMG

151. MIKAKO MIHASHI "GRACE"
ART DIRECTION : CHITTO
YEAR OF RELEASE : 1990
RECORD CO. : VIVID(JAPAN)
RECORD NO. : JC-003

**152. HORSES WITHOUT HEADS
"WHAT'S YOUR NAME(REMIX)"**
DESIGN : LAURENCE DUNMORE
YEAR OF RELEASE : 1990
RECORD CO. : POLYDOR

153. CATHY DENNIS "MOVE TO THIS"
YEAR OF RELEASE : 1990
RECORD CO. : POLYDOR

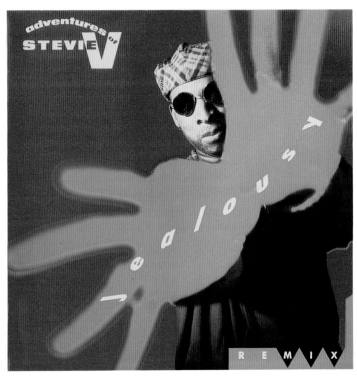

**149. ADVENTURES OF STEVIE V
"JEALOUSY REMIX"**
DESIGN : DAVID WATSON DAVID CROW
PHOTOGRAPHY : SIMON FOWLER
YEAR OF RELEASE : 1991
RECORD CO. : PHONOGRAM

150. ADVENTURES OF STEVIE V "JEALOUSY"
DESIGN : DAVID WATSON, DAVID CROW
PHOTOGRAPHY : SIMON FOWLER
YEAR OF RELEASE : 1991
RECORD CO. : PHONOGRAM

MIKAKO
MIHASHI

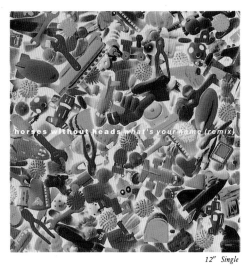

12" Single

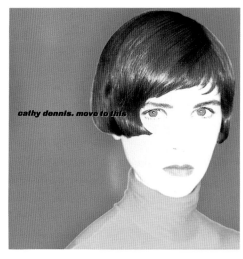

CD Single Front & Back

154. LIO "THE GIRL FROM IPANEMA"
DESIGN : ANTONIE CHOQUE
PHOTOGRAPHY : FRÉDÉRIQUE VEYSSET
PALETTE GRAPHIQUE : DENIS GIRAULT
YEAR OF RELEASE : 1990
RECORD CO. : POLYDOR

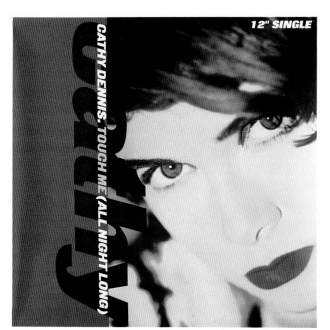

155. CATHY DENNIS
"TOUCH ME(ALL NIGHT LONG)"
YEAR OF RELEASE : 1990
RECORD CO. : POLYDOR

12" Single

electribe 101
inside out (remix)

Inside: **Inside out (mcm mix)**, produced by electribe 101 remixed by mcthurn, cutsworth / squirock written by j. rae published by mca music ltd
Outside = **inside out (pop mix)**, produced and mixed by electribe 101 written by j. rae published by mca music ltd
Outside = **Mummy I'm sick, I'm underwater** produced and mixed by electribe 101 written by b.r martin / s.a. fleming / j.j. stevens / r. omatosh / b.j. nordhoff published by phonogram music ltd
Sleeve by 3a photography by kate garner original version taken from the album "electribal memories"

Original sound recording made by phonogram ltd (London) - 1990 phonogram ltd (London) all rights reserved, unauthorised copying, reproduction
hiring, lending, public performance and broadcasting prohibited - 1990 phonogram ltd (London).

12" Single

156. ELECTRIBE 101 "INSIDE OUT (REMIX)"
DESIGN : 3A
PHOTOGRAPHY : KATE GARNER
YEAR OF RELEASE : 1990
RECORD CO. : PHONOGRAM

157. PETER BLEGVAD
"KING STRUT & OTHER STORIES"
ART DIRECTION : PB & JE
DESIGN : PB & JE
PHOTOGRAPHY : JAMES HAMILTON
YEAR OF RELEASE : 1990
RECORD CO. : ALFA(JAPAN)
RECORD NO. : ALCB-153

12" Single

158. ELECTRIBE 101 "INSIDE OUT"
DESIGN : 3A
PHOTOGRAPHY : KATE GARNER
YEAR OF RELEASE : 1990
RECORD CO. : PHONOGRAM

159. ENYA
ART DIRECTION : TOSHIE SOMA
PHOTOGRAPHY : MASATOMO KURIYA
RECORD CO. : BBC/JIMCO(JAPAN)
RECORD NO. : JIM 0001

160. KATE BUSH "THE SENSUAL WORLD"
DESIGN : KINDLIGHT, BILL SMITH STUDIO
PHOTOGRAPHY : JOHN CARDER BUSH, KINDLIGHT
YEAR OF RELEASE : 1989
RECORD CO. : EMI/TOSHIBA EMI(JAPAN)
RECORD NO. : TOCP-5924

161. PETER MURPHY "DEEP"

ART DIRECTION : PETER MURPHY
PHOTOGRAPHY : PAUL COX
CALLIGRAPHY : CHRIS BIGG
LOGO DESIGN : CHRIS BIGG
YEAR OF RELEASE : 1989
RECORD CO. : BEGGARS BANQUET/ALFA(JAPAN)
RECORD NO. : 29B2-112

鮎川 誠

162. MAKOTO AYUKAWA "KOOL-SOLO"

ART DIRECTION : KOICHI HARA
DESIGN : MASAO HIRUMA
PHOTOGRAPHY : DAISUKE YAMAGUCHI
YEAR OF RELEASE : 1990
RECORD CO. : ALFA(JAPAN)
RECORD NO. : ALCA-15

163. PRINCE AND THE REVOLUTION "PARADE"

ART DIRECTION : LAURA LIPUMA, JEFFREY KENT AYEROFF
DESIGN : LAURA LIPUMA
PHOTOGRAPHY : JEFF KATZ
YEAR OF RELEASE : 1986
RECORD CO. : WARNER/WARNER PIONEER(JAPAN)
RECORD NO. : 20P2-2614

164. PETER GABRIEL "SO"

DESIGN : PETER SAVILLE, BRETT WICKENS
PHOTOGRAPHY : TREVOR KEY
YEAR OF RELEASE : 1986
RECORD CO. : CHARISMA/VIRGIN JAPAN(JAPAN)
RECORD NO. : VJD-32010

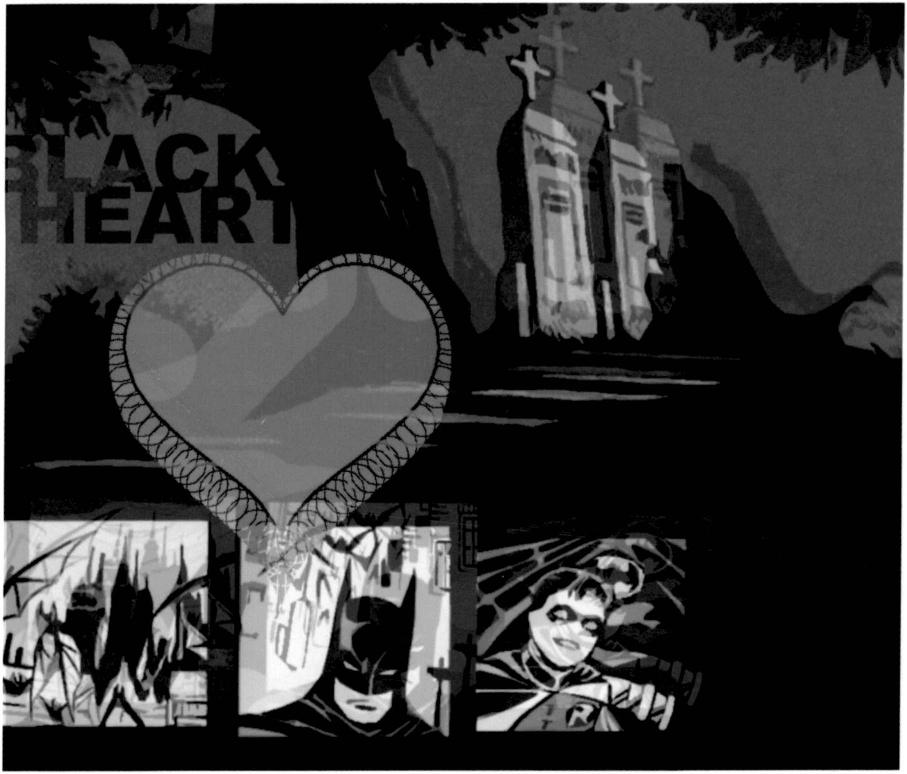
BLACK
HEART

165. THEN JERICO "THE BIG AREA"
DESIGN : NEXUS/SHAW
PHOTOGRAPHY : ROBERT ERDMAN, RAY ROBINSON
ILLUSTRATION : NEXUS
YEAR OF RELEASE : 1989
RECORD CO. : LONDON/POLYDOR(JAPAN)
RECORD NO. : POOL 20110

166. JOHN CALE "SABOTAGE/LIVE"
ART DIRECTION : JOHN VOGEL
PHOTOGRAPHY : HUGH BROWN
YEAR OF RELEASE : 1979
RECORD CO. : SPY

167. BAUHAUS "THE SKY'S GONE OUT"
DESIGN : BAUHAUS
ILLUSTRATION : BAUHAUS
YEAR OF RELEASE : 1982
RECORD CO. : BEGGARS BANQUET/COLUMBIA(JAPAN)
RECORD NO. : 18B2-119

168. DISCHARGE
   "HEAR NOTHING SEE NOTHING SAY NOTHING"
DESIGN : CAL
PHOTOGRAPHY : BIFFO GASMASK
YEAR OF RELEASE : 1982
RECORD CO. : CLAY/VAP(JAPAN)
RECORD NO. : 85013-30

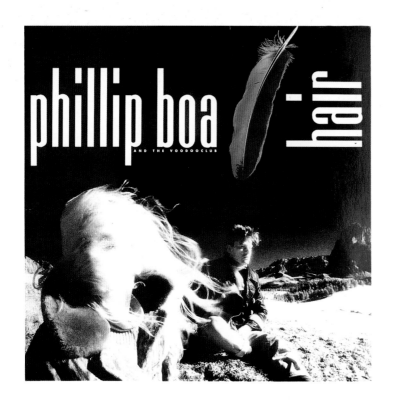

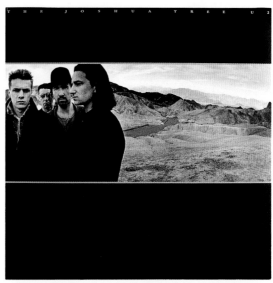

169. PHILLIP BOA AND THE VOODOOCLUB "HAIR"
DESIGN : DIRK RUDOLPH
PHOTOGRAPHY : DIRK RUDOLPH
YEAR OF RELEASE : 1989
RECORD CO. : POLYDOR/POLYDOR(JAPAN)
RECORD NO. : POOP-20248

170. THE ALARM "ELECTRIC FOLKLORE LIVE"
ART DIRECTION : NICK EGAN
DESIGN : TRACY VEAL
PHOTOGRAPHY : EBET ROBERTS, CARY LANDER
YEAR OF RELEASE : 1988
RECORD CO. : I.R.S./VICTOR(JAPAN)
RECORD NO. : VDP-1425

171. U2 "THE JOSHUA TREE"
ART DIRECTION : THE CREATIVE DEPT
DESIGN : STEVE AVERILL
PHOTOGRAPHY : ANTON CORBIJN
YEAR OF RELEASE : 1987
RECORD CO. : ISLAND/POLYSTAR(JAPAN)
RECORD NO. : P24D-10053

172. U2 "RATTLE AND HUM"
DESIGN : DZN
PHOTOGRAPHY : ANTON CORBIJN
YEAR OF RELEASE : 1988
RECORD CO. : ISLAND/POLYSTAR(JAPAN)
RECORD NO. : P33D-20075

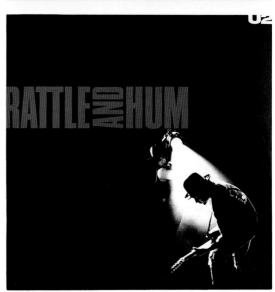

173. DEPECHE MODE "101"
ART DIRECTION : PAUL WEST
DESIGN : PETER SAVILLE ASSOCIATES
PHOTOGRAPHY : ANTON CORBIJN

174. RYUICHI SAKAMOTO "BEAUTY"
ART DIRECTION : ROBERT BERGMAN-UNGAR
COVER CONCEPT : NORIKA SORA FOR KAB INC.
PHOTOGRAPHY : ALBERT WATSON
YEAR OF RELEASE : 1989
RECORD CO. : VIRGIN / VIRGIN(JAPAN)
RECORD NO. : VJD-32235

175. THIS MORTAL COIL
DESIGN : 23 ENVELOPE
RECORD CO. : 4AD/COLUMBIA(JAPAN)
RECORD NO. : CY-4411

Front

176. DAVID SYLVIAN, HOLGER CZUKAY
"PLIGHT & PREMONITION"
DESIGN : YUKA FUJII

PHOTOGRAPHY : YUKA FUJII

YEAR OF RELEASE : 1988

RECORD CO. : VIRGIN/VIRGIN(JAPAN)

RECORD NO. : VJD-32045

Back & Front

177. PATTI SMITH "DREAM OF LIFE"
PHOTOGRAPHY : ROBERT MAPPLETHORPE

YEAR OF RELEASE : 1988

RECORD CO. : ARISTA/BMG VICTOR(JAPAN)

RECORD NO. : A32D-52

178. YAZOO "YOU AND ME BOTH"
DESIGN : 23 ENVELOPE
YEAR OF RELEASE : 1983
RECORD CO. : MUTE/WARNER PIONEER(JAPAN)
RECORD NO. : 18P2-2679

179. RUSH "PRESTO"
ART DIRECTION : HUGH SYME
PHOTOGRAPHY : SCARPATI
YEAR OF RELEASE : 1989
RECORD CO. : ATLANTIC/MMG(JAPAN)
RECORD NO. : AMCY-4

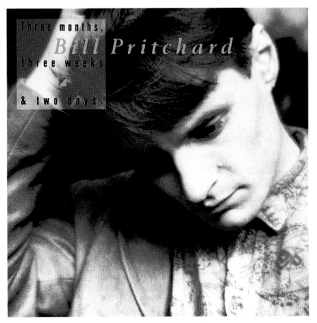

180. BILL PRITCHARD
"THREE MONTH, THREE WEEKS AND TWO DAYS"
DESIGN : JOËL VAN AUDENHAEGE
PHOTOGRAPHY : DANNY WILLEMS
YEAR OF RELEASE : 1990
RECORD CO. : A PLAY IT AGAIN SAM/JIMCO(JAPAN)
RECORD NO. : CMJ-7001

181. PATRICK O'HEARN "RIVERS GONNA RISE"
ART DIRECTION : NORMAN MOORE
DESIGN : NORMAN MOORE
PHOTOGRAPHY : ROBERT TORBET
YEAR OF RELEASE : 1988
RECORD CO. : PRIVATE MUSIC

184. MAE MCKENNA "MIRAGE AND REALITY"
YEAR OF RELEASE : 1990
RECORD CO. : VIRGIN/VIRGIN(JAPAN)
RECORD NO. : VJCP-57

182. MAZZY STAR "SHE HANGS BRIGHTLY"
DESIGN : SERPENT RECORDS
YEAR OF RELEASE : 1990
RECORD CO. : ROUGH TRADE/VICTOR(JAPAN)
RECORD NO. : VICP-72

183. BAUHAUS
"SWING THE HEARTACHE THE BBC SESSIONS"
ART DIRECTION : STIFF WEAPON
DESIGN : STIFF WEAPON
PHOTOGRAPHY : TANSY SPINKS
YEAR OF RELEASE : 1989
RECORD CO. : BEGGARS BANQUET

185. PIXIES "COME ON PILGRIM"
ART DIRECTION : VAUGHAN OLIVER
DESIGN : VAUGHAN OLIVER
PHOTOGRAPHY : SIMON LARBALESTIER
YEAR OF RELEASE : 1987
RECORD CO. : 4AD

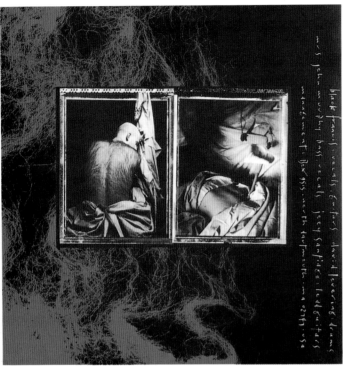

12" Single Back

12" Single Front

12" Single

186. PIXIES "DOOLITTLE"
ART DIRECTION : VAUGHAM OLIVER/V 23
DESIGN : VAUGHAM OLIVER/V 23
PHOTOGRAPHY : SIMON LARBALESTIER
RECORD CO. : 4AD/COLUMBIA(JAPAN)
RECORD NO. : CY-3531

187. PIXIES "BOSSANOVA"
ART DIRECTION : VAUGHAN OLIVER/V 23
DESIGN : VAUGHAN OLIVER/V 23
PHOTOGRAPHY : SIMON LARBALESTIER
RECORD CO. : 4AD/COLUMBIA(JAPAN)
RECORD NO. : COCY-6628

188. PIXIES "DIG FOR FIRE"
ART DIRECTION : VAUGHAN OLIVER/V23.
PHOTOGRAPHY : SIMON LARBALESTIER
YEAR OF RELEASE : 1990
RECORD CO. : 4AD

189. THE SUNDAYS
"READING, WRITING AND ARITHMETIC"
DESIGN : THE SUNDAYS, DESIGNLAND
SLEEVE : MATT VARNISH
YEAR OF RELEASE : 1990
RECORD CO. : ROUGH TRADE/VICTOR(JAPAN)
RECORD NO. : VICP-19

190. COCTEAU TWINS "BLUE BELL KNOLL"
DESIGN : PAUL WEST, JEREMY TILSTON
PHOTOGRAPHY : JURGEN TELLER
YEAR OF RELEASE : 1988
RECORD CO. : 4AD/COLUMBIA(JAPAN)
RECORD NO. : 25CY-2637

191. HAROLD BUDD, SIMON RAYMONDE,
ROBIN GUTHRIE, ELIZABETH FRASER
"THE MOON AND THE MELODIES"
DESIGN : 23 ENVELOPE
RECORD CO. : 4AD/COLUMBIA(JAPAN)
RECORD NO. : CY-4414

  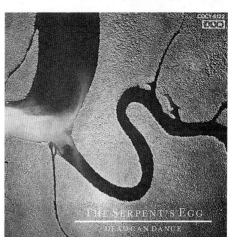

192. CLAN OF XYMOX "MEDUSA"
PHOTOGRAPHY : NIGEL GLIERSON
YEAR OF RELEASE : 1990
RECORD CO. : 4AD/COLUMBIA(JAPAN)
RECORD NO. : CY-4656

193. COCTEAU TWINS "THE PINK OPAQUE"
DESIGN : 23 ENVELOPE
PHOTOGRAPHY : 23 ENVELOPE
YEAR OF RELEASE : 1985
RECORD CO. : 4AD/COLUMBIA(JAPAN)
RECORD NO. : CY-4508

194. DEAD CAN DANCE "THE SERPENT'S EGG"
YEAR OF RELEASE : 1988
RECORD CO. : 4AD/COLUMBIA(JAPAN)
RECORD NO. : COCY-6122

195. SONNY SOUTHON
"FALLING THROUGH A CLOUD"
ART DIRECTION : MELANIE NISSEN
DESIGN : TRACY VEAL
PHOTOGRAPHY : MELANIE NISSEN
YEAR OF RELEASE : 1990
RECORD CO. : CHARISMA/VIRGIN(JAPAN)
RECORD NO. : VJCP-49

196. ZABADAK "THOIONGAKU"
ART DIRECTION : ATSUSHI EBINA
DESIGN : ATSUSHI EBINA
PHOTO COLLAGE : ATSUSHI EBINA
YEAR OF RELEASE : 1991
RECORD CO. : MMG(JAPAN)
RECORD NO. : AMCM-4084

197. ASSOCIATES POPERA
"THE SINGLES COLLECTION"
PHOTOGRAPHY : RICHARD HAUGHTON
YEAR OF RELEASE : 1990
RECORD CO. : WEA

 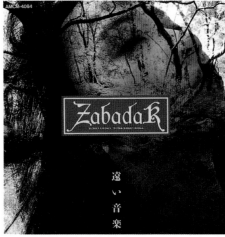 

198. GIANNI NOCENZI "EMPUSA"
ART DIRECTION : ANDREW W. ELLIS
DESIGN : ICON
PHOTOGRAPHY : LUCIANO VELLETTA
ILLUSTRATION : FERNANDO BIRRI
YEAR OF RELEASE : 1989
RECORD CO. : VIRGIN/VIRGIN(JAPAN)
RECORD NO. : VJD-5016

199. SURBAND "CANTICO"
COVER : MIX BREMEN TORSTEN HÖNER
DESIGN : ECKHARD MÖLLER GRAFIKDESIGN BREMEN
PHOTOGRAPHY : ULI BALSS
RECORD CO. : JARO

200. SHADOWFAX "THE ODD GET EVEN"
ART DIRECTION : NORMAN MOORE
DESIGN : NORMAN MOORE
PHOTOGRAPHY : MERLYN ROSENBERG
YEAR OF RELEASE : 1990
RECORD CO. : PRIVATE MUSIC

201. ALL ABOUT EVE
  "SCARLET AND OTHER STORIES"
ART DIRECTION : STYLOROUGE
DESIGN : STYLOROUGE
PHOTOGRAPHY : HOLLY WARBURTON
YEAR OF RELEASE : 1989
RECORD CO. : PHONOGRAM
/PHONOGRAM(JAPAN)
RECORD NO. : PPD-1090

202. ANNIE HASLAM
ART DIRECTION : STACY DRUMMOND
PHOTOGRAPHY : HOLLY WARBURTON
RECORD CO. : VIRGIN/VIRGIN(JAPAN)
RECORD NO. : VJCP-56

203. KUROYURI SHIMAI
  "SAIGO WA TENSHI TO KIKU
  SHIZUMU SEKAI NO HANE NO KIOKU"
DESIGN : CRYPTOMEN
PHOTOGRAPHY : HOLLY WARBURTON
ILLUSTRATION : JUNKO KAWAMOTO
YEAR OF RELEASE : 1990
RECORD CO. : SSE COMMUNICATIONS(JAPAN)
RECORD NO. : SSE 4003

204. DANNY WILSON "BEBOP MOPTOP"
DESIGN : BREEDEN
PHOTOGRAPHY : BREEDEN
YEAR OF RELEASE : 1989
RECORD CO. : VIRGIN/VIRGIN(JAPAN)
RECORD NO. : VJD-32221

205. RENAISSANCE "TALES OF 1001 NIGHTS"
ART DIRECTION : MARGO CHASE
DESIGN : LORNA STOVALL
PHOTOGRAPHY : SIDNEY COOPER, MARGO CHASE
YEAR OF RELEASE : 1990
RECORD CO. : SIRE

206. BILL FRISELL "IS THAT YOU?"
ART DIRECTION : MANHATTAN DESIGN
DESIGN : MANHATTAN DESIGN
PHOTOGRAPHY : STEPHEN FRAILEY
YEAR OF RELEASE : 1990
RECORD CO. : ELEKTRA/WEA(JAPAN)
RECORD NO. : WPCP-4041

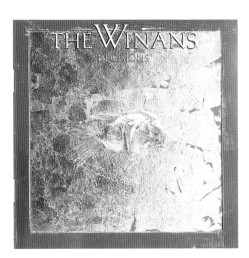

12" Single

207. THE WINANS "DECISIONS"
ART DIRECTION : MARY ANN DIBS
PHOTOGRAPHY : RUSSELL COMFORT
COLLAGE : MARY ANN DIBS
YEAR OF RELEASE : 1987
RECORD CO. : QWEST

208. BREATHLESS "ALWAYS · FLOWERS DIE"
PHOTOGRAPHY : KEVIN WESTENBERG
YEAR OF RELEASE : 1990
RECORD CO. : TENOR · VOSSA

209. THE CREATURES "BOOMERANG"
YEAR OF RELEASE : 1990
RECORD CO. : POLYDOR/POLYDOR(JAPAN)
RECORD NO. : POOP 20318

210. NEWEST MODEL "CROSSBREEDPARK"
ART DIRECTION : TAKASHI NAKAGAWA
DESIGN : YASUNORI ARAI
PHOTOGRAPHY : TAKUYA KIMURA, YASUNORI ARAI
YEAR OF RELEASE : 1990
RECORD CO. : KING(JAPAN)
RECORD NO. : KICS 30

Back & Front

211. DEACON BLUE "OOH LAS VEGAS"
DESIGN : BRIDGES & WOODS
PHOTOGRAPHY : ELIZABETH LYND
YEAR OF RELEASE : 1990
RECORD CO. : CBS/EPIC SONY(JAPAN)
RECORD NO. : ESCA 5181〜2

Front cover & Inside spreads

212. DEPECHE MODE "VIOLATOR"
DESIGN : AREA
PHOTOGRAPHY : ANTON CORBIJN
YEAR OF RELEASE : 1990
RECORD CO. : MUTE/ALFA(JAPAN)
RECORD NO. : ALCB-35

213. PHILLIP BOA AND THE VOODOOCLUB
 "BOA HISPANOLA"
DESIGN : DIRK RUDOLPH
PHOTOGRAPHY : DIRK RUDOLPH
RECORD CO. : POLYDOR/POLYDOR(JAPAN)
RECORD NO. : POCP-1019

214. STAN GETZ "APASIONADO"
ART DIRECTION : CHUCK BEESON
DESIGN : CHUCK BEESON
PHOTOGRAPHY : DEAN CHAMBERLAIN
YEAR OF RELEASE : 1990
RECORD CO. : A & M/PONY CANYON(JAPAN)
RECORD NO. : PCCY-10133

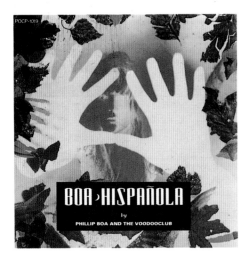

215. SQUEEZE "FRANK"
DESIGN : STYLOROUGE
PHOTOGRAPHY : TREVOR ROGERS
YEAR OF RELEASE : 1989
RECORD CO. : A & M/PONY CANION(JAPAN)
RECORD NO. : PCCY-10016

216. THE DREAM ACADEMY "LOVE"
PHOTOGRAPHY : LANGLEY IDDINS
YEAR OF RELEASE : 1990
RECORD CO. : WEA

12"

217. RIDE " SMILE "
YEAR OF RELEASE : 1990
RECORD CO. : SIRE/WARNER PIONEER(JAPAN)
RECORD NO. : WPCP-4061

218. RIDE "CHELSEA GIRL"
YEAR OF RELEASE : 1989
RECORD CO. : CREATION

219. RIDE "PLAY"
DESIGN : RIDE
PHOTOGRAPHY : LOU
YEAR OF RELEASE : 1990
RECORD CO. : CREATION

220. MORRISSEY "BONA DRAG"
ART DIRECTION : MORRISSEY
ART COORDINATION : JO SLEE
DESIGN : DESIGNLAND
PHOTOGRAPHY : JURGEN TELLER
YEAR OF RELEASE : 1990
RECORD CO. : EMI/TOSHIBA EMI(JAPAN)
RECORD NO. : TOCP-6472

221. AZTEC CAMERA "THE CRYING SCENE"
PHOTOGRAPHY : RICHARD BURNS
YEAR OF RELEASE : 1990
RECORD CO. : WEA

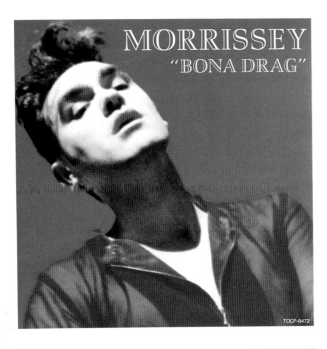

12" Single

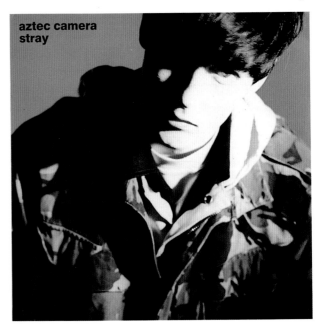

222. LITTLE CREATURES
ART DIRECTION : HIROSHI SUNTO
DESIGN : HIROSHI MITOBE
PHOTOGRAPHY : BRUCE OSBORN
YEAR OF RELEASE : 1990
RECORD CO. : MIDI(JAPAN)
RECORD NO. : MDC4-1122

223. AZTEC CAMERA "STRAY"
PHOTOGRAPHY : RICHARD BURNS
YEAR OF RELEASE : 1990
RECORD CO. : WEA/WEA(JAPAN)
RECORD NO. : WMC5-110

224. EURYTHMICS "WE TOO ARE ONE"
ART DIRECTION : LAURENCE STEVENS
DESIGN : LAURENCE STEVENS
PHOTOGRAPHY : JEAN BAPTISTE MONDINO
YEAR OF RELEASE : 1989
RECORD CO. : RCA/BMG VICTOR(JAPAN)
RECORD NO. : R32P-1212

**225. MARK SPRINGER, SARAH SARHANDI
"SWANS AND TURTLES"**
ART DIRECTION : ZOLTAN
DESIGN : ZOLTAN
YEAR OF RELEASE : 1990
RECORD CO. : VIRGIN

**226. ANDREW BERRY
"KISS ME I'M COLD(SAVE THE WHALE MIX)"**
YEAR OF RELEASE : 1990
RECORD CO. : PHONOGRAM

12" Single

12" Single

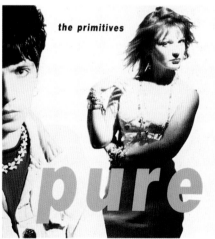

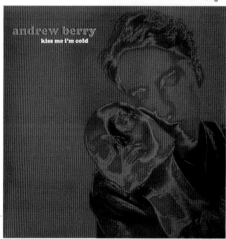

12" Single

227. WOP BOP TORLEDO "JUNGLE FEVER"
ART DIRECTION : JOHN WARWICKERVIVID ID
PHOTOGRAPHY : SATOSHI SAKUSA
YEAR OF RELEASE : 1990
RECORD CO. : CHARISMA

228. THE PRIMITIVES "PURE"
DESIGN : THE LEISURE PROCESS
PHOTOGRAPHY : PAUL COX
YEAR OF RELEASE : 1989
RECORD CO. : RCA/BMG VICTOR(JAPAN)
RECORD NO. : R32P-1235

229. ANDREW BERRY "KISS ME I'M COLD"
YEAR OF RELEASE : 1990
RECORD CO. : PHONOGRAM

230. TERENCE TRENT D'ARBY "TTD"

DESIGN : PETER BARRETT

PHOTOGRAPHY : SHEILA ROCK

YEAR OF RELEASE : 1987

RECORD CO. : EPIC/EPIC SONY(JAPAN)

RECORD NO. : 25•8P-5149

231. SAYURI KOKUSYO "SAKANA"

ART DIRECTION : YASUTAKA KATOH

DESIGN : YASUTAKA KATOH

PHOTOGRAPHY : KOH HOSOKAWA

YEAR OF RELEASE : 1989

RECORD CO. : CBS SONY(JAPAN)

RECORD NO. : CSCL-1026

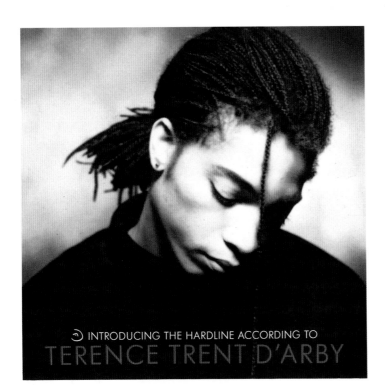

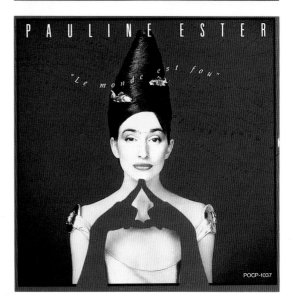

235. TRACY CHAPMAN
ART DIRECTION : CAROL BOBOLTS
PHOTOGRAPHY : MATT MAHURIN
YEAR OF RELEASE : 1988
RECORD CO. : ELEKTRA/WEA(JAPAN)
RECORD NO. : 25P2-2121

236. RIE MIYAZAWA "CHEPOP"
ART DIRECTION : HIRONORI KOMIYA
PHOTOGRAPHY : SACHIKO KURU
YEAR OF RELEASE : 1990
RECORD CO. : CBS SONY(JAPAN)
RECORD NO. : CSCL-1523

232. MINAKO TANAKA "GIMMMICK"
ART DIRECTION : REIKO NOTO(PUBLIX INC)
DESIGN : SOUSUKE(PUBLIX INC)
YEAR OF RELEASE : 1990
RECORD CO. : TOKUMA(JAPAN)
RECORD NO. : TKCA-30139

233. EMERGENCY "BON CHIC"
ART DIRECTION : AKIO SAKASHITA
DESIGN : AKIO SAKASHITA, KENJI WATABE
PHOTOGRAPHY : TOSHITAKA NIWA
YEAR OF RELEASE : 1990
RECORD CO. : HUMMING BIRD(JAPAN)
RECORD NO. : HBCL-5001

234. PAULINE ESTER "LE MONDE EST FOU"
ART DIRECTION : JEAN-PIERRE HAIE
DESIGN : NOUS Z AND CIE
PHOTOGRAPHY : GILLES CAPPE
YEAR OF RELEASE : 1990
RECORD CO. : POLYDOR/POLYDOR(JAPAN)
RECORD NO. : POCP-1037

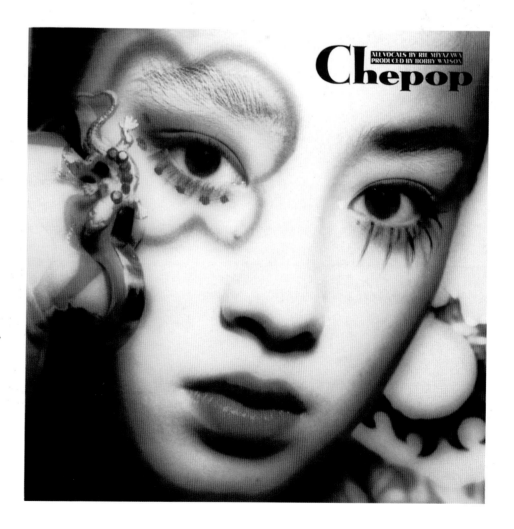

二十世紀
少年読本

237. "CIRCUS BOYS SONG BOOK"
ART DIRECTION : YASUTAKA KATO
PHOTOGRAPHY : HARUHI FUJI
YEAR OF RELEASE : 1989
RECORD CO. : CBS SONY(JAPAN)
RECORD NO. : CSCL 1023

238. YOSHIYUKI OHSAWA "RAKUEN"
ART DIRECTION : NOBUAKI TAKAHASHI
DESIGN : NOBUAKI TAKAHASHI
PHOTOGRAPHY : NAOTO OHKAWA
YEAR OF RELEASE : 1990
RECORD CO. : EPIC SONY(JAPAN)
RECORD NO. : ESCB 1103

239. BUCK-TICK "AKUNOHANA"
DESIGN : KEN SAKAGUCHI
PHOTOGRAPHY : BRUNO DAYAN
YEAR OF RELEASE : 1990
RECORD CO. : VICTOR(JAPAN)
RECORD NO. : VICL-2

240. KRONOS QUARTET "BLACK ANGELS"
ART DIRECTION : MANHATTAN DESIGN
DESIGN : MANHATTAN DESIGN
PHOTOGRAPHY : MATT MAHURIN
YEAR OF RELEASE : 1990
RECORD CO. : ELEKTRA
/WARNER PIONEER(JAPAN)
RECORD NO. : WPCC-3656

241. LEAD INTO GOLD
"CHICKS & SPEED:FUTURISM"
DESIGN : BRIAN SHANLEY
YEAR OF RELEASE : 1990
RECORD CO. : SPURBURN. BMI.

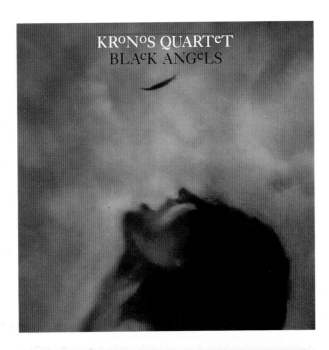

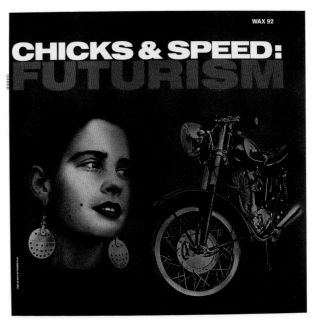

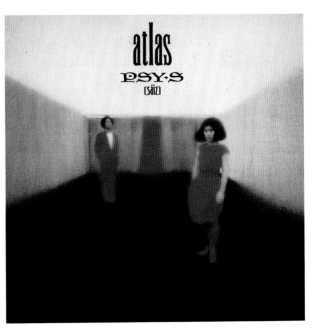

242. MINAKO YOSHIDA "GAZER"
ART DIRECTION : YOHKO HAMADA
DESIGN : YOHKO HAMADA
PHOTOGRAPHY : RYUICHI OSHIMOTO
YEAR OF RELEASE : 1990
RECORD CO. : SOHBI(JAPAN)
RECORD NO. : SHB-1007

243. PSY·S "ATLAS"
ART DIRECTION : HIROSHI OOKI
DESIGN : HIROSHI OOKI
PHOTOGRAPHY : TERUO IWAMOTO
PHOTO EFFECTED : MOTOKI TSUSHIMA
YEAR OF RELEASE : 1989
RECORD CO. : CBS SONY(JAPAN)
RECORD NO. : 32DH-5280

244. THE SMITHS "THE QUEEN IS DEAD"
ART DIRECTION : MORRISSEY
DESIGN : CARYN GOUGH
YEAR OF RELEASE : 1986
RECORD CO. : ROUGH TRADE/VICTOR(JAPAN)
RECORD NO. : 32JC-162

**245. THE BEAUTIFUL SOUTH
"WELCOME TO THE BEAUTIFUL SOUTH"**
PHOTOGRAPHY : JAN SAUDEK
YEAR OF RELEASE : 1989
RECORD CO. : GO!/POLYDOR(JAPAN)
RECORD NO. : POOL-20135

246. XTC "DEAR GOD"
PHOTOGRAPHY : CAVIN COCHRANE
YEAR OF RELEASE : 1987
RECORD CO. : VIRGIN

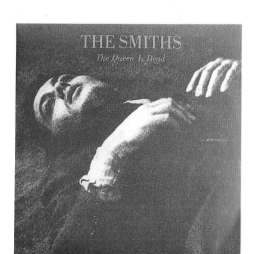

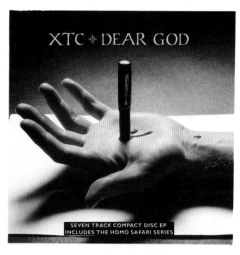

12" Single

247. THE SMITHS "SHEILA TAKE A BOW"
ART DIRECTION : MORRISSEY
DESIGN : CARYN GOUGH
YEAR OF RELEASE : 1987
RECORD CO. : ROUGH TRADE

248. IN TUA NUA "THE LONG ACRE"
ART DIRECTION : GARY WATHEN
DESIGN : ICON
PHOTOGRAPHY : TIM O'SULLIVAN
YEAR OF RELEASE : 1988
RECORD CO. : VIRGIN/VIRGIN(JAPAN)
RECORD NO. : VJD-32084

249. THE CALL "RECONCILED"
ART DIRECTION : CAROL FRIEDMAN
DESIGN : JANET PERR
PHOTOGRAPHY : WESTERN HISTORY COLLECTION
YEAR OF RELEASE : 1986
RECORD CO. : ELEKTRA

250. THE KNACK "SERIOUS FUN"
ART DIRECTION : STEVE SAMIOF
DESIGN : MIKE FINK/HEIGHT
PHOTOGRAPHY : KAREN FILTER
YEAR OF RELEASE : 1991
RECORD CO. : CHARISMA/VIRGIN(JAPAN)
RECORD NO. : VJCP-28023

251. JELLY FISH "BELLY BUTTON"
ART DIRECTION : MICK HAGGERTY, STEVE SAMIOF
DESIGN : MICK HAGGERY
PHOTOGRAPHY : PETER DARLEY MILLER
YEAR OF RELEASE : 1990
RECORD CO. : CHARISMA/VIRGIN(JAPAN)
RECORD NO. : VJCP-48

255. RITA MITSOUKO
   "LES RITA(RE) MITSOUKO"
DESIGN : JUDITH E. CHRIST
PHOTOGRAPHY : STEPHANE SEDNAOUI
YEAR OF RELEASE : 1990
RECORD CO. : VIRGIN

256. NAJA "CHI CHO HOI"
ART DIRECTION : TAKI ONO
DESIGN : TAKI ONO
PHOTOGRAPHY : PETER GRAVELLE
YEAR OF RELEASE : 1989
RECORD CO. : POLYSTAR(JAPAN)
RECORD NO. : H30R-10006

257. DICK LEE "ASIAMAJOR"
DESIGN : DICK LEE
PHOTOGRAPHY : GARY SNG
YEAR OF RELEASE : 1990
RECORD CO. : WEA(JAPAN)
RECORD NO. : WMC5-169

252. TEARS FOR FEARS "THE SEEDS OF LOVE"
ART DIRECTION : DAVID SCHEINMANN/AVID IMAGES
ART WORK : STYLOROUGE
PHOTOGRAPHY : DAVID SCHEINMANN/AVID IMAGES
YEAR OF RELEASE : 1989
RECORD CO. : POLYGRAM/PHONOGRAM(JAPAN)
RECORD NO. : PPD-1060

253. L'AFFAIRE LOUIS TRIO "SANS LEGENDO"
PHOTOGRAPHY : THIERRY MERCADAL
YEAR OF RELEASE : 1990
RECORD CO. : BARCLAY

254. STEVE VAI "PASSION AND WARFARE"
ART DIRECTION : STEVE VAI, DAVE BATT, BILL REIM
ART WORK : AARON BROWN
PHOTOGRAPHY : JIM HAGOPIAN
YEAR OF RELEASE : 1990
RECORD CO. : RELATIVITY/CBS SONY(JAPAN)
RECORD NO. : CSCS-5180

258. RUFUS THOMAS
"THAT WOMAN IS POISEN!"
DESIGN : PETER AMFT
PHOTOGRAPHY : PETER AMFT
YEAR OF RELEASE : 1988
RECORD CO. : ALLIGATOR/CENTURY(JAPAN)
RECORD NO. : 25ED-6011

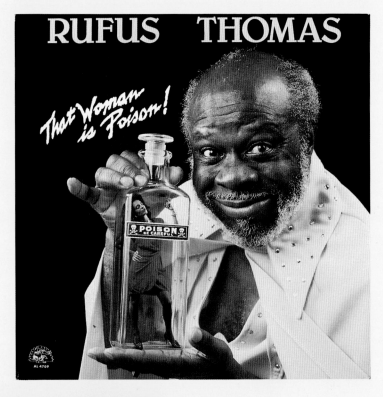

259. THE DIABOLICAL BIZ MARKIE
"THE BIZ NEVER SLEEPS"
ART DIRECTION : GEORGE DuBOSE
DESIGN : GEORGE DuBOSE
YEAR OF RELEASE : 1989
RECORD CO. : WARNER/WARNER PIONEER(JAPAN)
RECORD NO. : WPCP-3457

260. SHABBA RANKS "RAPPIN' WITH THE LADIES"
DESIGN : TONY MCDERMOTT
PHOTOGRAPHY : DAVID CORIO
YEAR OF RELEASE : 1990
RECORD CO. : GREENSLEEVES

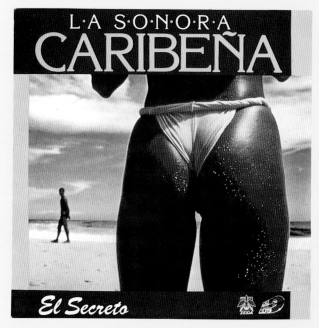

261. L·A S·O·N·O·R·A "CARIBEÑA"
RECORD CO. : ZEIDA

262. THE 2 LIVE CREW
"AS NASTY AS THEY WANNA BE"
DESIGN : MILTON MIZELL
PHOTOGRAPHY : MACK HARTSHORN
YEAR OF RELEASE : 1989
RECORD CO. : LUKE/TEICHIKU(JAPAN)
RECORD NO. : TECP-25527

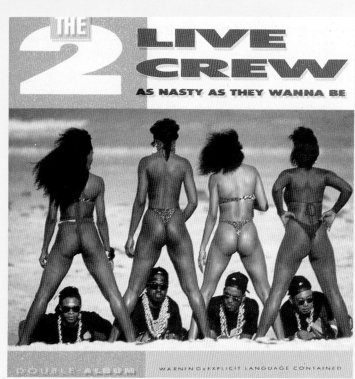

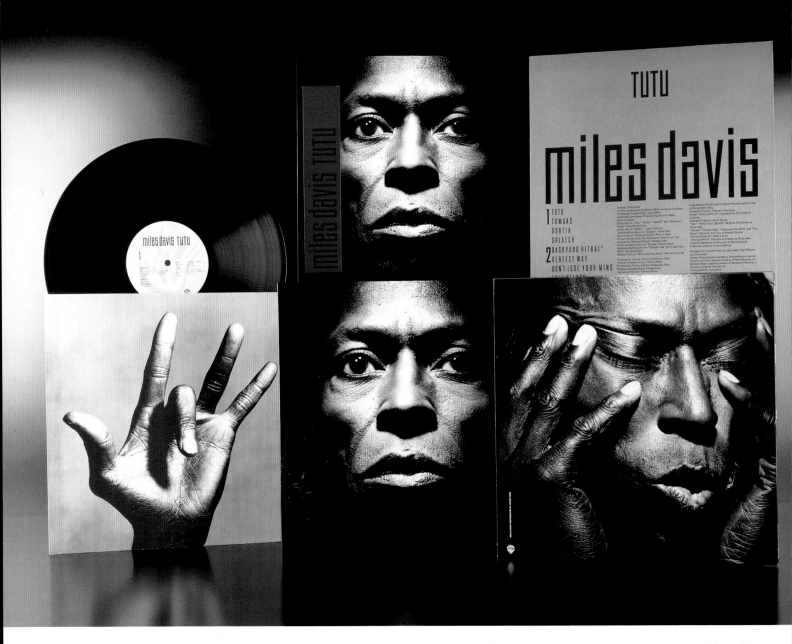

263. MILES DAVIS "TUTU"
ART DIRECTION : EIKO ISHIOKA
DESIGN : SUSAN WELT
PHOTOGRAPHY : LRVING PENN
YEAR OF RELEASE : 1987
RECORD CO. : WARNER
/WARNER PIONEER(JAPAN)
RECORD NO. : WPCP-3568

264. DEATH IN JUNE
DESIGN : NER/SUPERNATURAL ORGANIZATION
PHOTOGRAPHY : DOUGLAS P
YEAR OF RELEASE : 1989
RECORD CO. : A SUPERNATURAL ORGANIZATION(JAPAN)
RECORD NO. : SUR MLP11

265. PHILIP GLASS
"MISHIMA ORIGINAL MUSIC COMPOSED"
ART DIRECTION : EIKO ISHIOKA
DESIGN : MAKOTO KUMAKURA
PHOTOGRAPHY : MASAYOSHI SUKITA
YEAR OF RELEASE : 1985
RECORD CO. : ELEKTRA ASYLUM NONESUCH

266. SHIRLEY HORN "ALL OF ME"
ART DIRECTION : YASUTAKA KATO
PHOTOGRAPHY : KOH HOSOKAWA
YEAR OF RELEASE : 1987
RECORD CO. : CBS SONY(JAPAN)
RECORD NO. : 32DP-683

267. SUSANNAH MCCORKLE
"AS TIME GOES BY"
ART DIRECTION : YASUTAKA KATO
PHOTOGRAPHY : SHIN GINUSHI
YEAR OF RELEASE : 1987
RECORD CO. : CBS SONY(JAPAN)
RECORD NO. : 32DP-685

268. CARMEN LUNDY "NIGHT AND DAY"
ART DIRECTION : YASUTAKA KATO
PHOTOGRAPHY : SHIGERU BANDO
YEAR OF RELEASE : 1987
RECORD CO. : CBS SONY(JAPAN)
RECORD NO. : 32DP-690

269. CAROL SLOANE "BUT NOT FOR ME"

ART DIRECTION : YASUTAKA KATO
PHOTOGRAPHY : KHO HOSOKAWA
YEAR OF RELEASE : 1987
RECORD CO. : CBS SONY(JAPAN)·
RECORD NO. : 32DP-681

270. MILLIE VERNON "OVER THE RAINBOW"

ART DIRECTION : YASUTAKA KATO
PHOTOGRAPHY : KHO HOSOKAWA
YEAR OF RELEASE : 1987
RECORD CO. : CBS SONY(JAPAN)
RECORD NO. : 32DP-689

271. SHEILA JORDAN "BODY AND SOUL"

272. EDDIE GOMEZ "MEZGO"
ART DIRECTION : EIKO ISHIOKA
DESIGN : EIKO ISHIOKA, MAKOTO KUMAKURA
PHOTOGRAPHY : KAZUMI KURIGAMI
YEAR OF RELEASE : 1986
RECORD CO. : EPIC SONY(JAPAN)
RECORD NO. : 32•8H-65

Front & Back

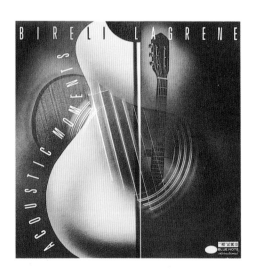

273. BIRELI LAGRENE
"ACOUSTIC MOMENTS"
DESIGN : JANET PERR
PHOTOGRAPHY : GEOFF SPEAR
YEAR OF RELEASE : 1991
RECORD CO. : BLUE NOTE

274. GRANT GEISSMAN "TAKE ANOTHER LOOK"
ART DIRECTION : KATHLEEN COVERT
DESIGN : KATHLEEN COVERT
PHOTOGRAPHY : DAN ARSENAULT
YEAR OF RELEASE : 1990
RECORD CO. : BLUEMOON

**275. GARY THOMAS AND SEVENTH QUADRANT
"BY ANY MEANS NECESSARY"**
DESIGN : STEVE BYRAM
PHOTOGRAPHY : ROBERT LEWIS
YEAR OF RELEASE : 1989
RECORD CO. : POLYDOR(JAPAN)
RECORD NO. : JOOJ-20352

**276. GARY THOMAS
"WHILE THE GATE IS OPEN"**
DESIGN : MYX
PHOTOGRAPHY : ROBERT LEWIS
YEAR OF RELEASE : 1990
RECORD CO. : POLYDOR(JAPAN)
RECORD NO. : JOOJ-20352

277. SUZANNE CIANI "PIANISSIMO"
ART DIRECTION : MELANIE PENNY
DESIGN : MARGO CHASE
PHOTOGRAPHY : DIANE RUBINGER
ILLUSTRATION : ROBBIE CAVOLINA
YEAR OF RELEASE : 1990
RECORD CO. : PRIVATE MUSIC
/BMG VICTOR(JAPAN)
RECORD NO. : BVCP-113

278. ANDY SUMMERS "CHARMING SNAKES"
ART DIRECTION : NORMAN MOORE
DESIGN : NORMAN MOORE
PHOTOGRAPHY : MERLYN ROSENBERG
YEAR OF RELEASE : 1990
RECORD CO. : PRIVATE MUSIC
/BMG VICTOR(JAPAN)
RECORD NO. : BVCP-27

279. BREATHE "PEACE OF MIND"
ART DIRECTION : JOHN WARWICKER
PHOTOGRAPHY : MARTIN BRADING
YEAR OF RELEASE : 1990
RECORD CO. : VIRGIN/VIRGIN(JAPAN)
RECORD NO. : VJCP-2804

280. KIETH RICHARDS "TALK IS CHEAP"
ART DIRECTION : JEFF AYROFF, KEITH RICHARDS
DESIGN : VIRGIN ART LOS ANGELES
PHOTOGRAPHY : SANTÉD'ORAZIO
YEAR OF RELEASE : 1988
RECORD CO. : VIRGIN/VIRGIN(JAPAN)
RECORD NO. : VJD-32074

281. BERNIE WORRELL "FUNK OF AGES"
DESIGN : CHERMAYEFF & GEISMAR ASSOCIATES
PHOTOGRAPHY : SALLY ANDERSON BRUCE
YEAR OF RELEASE : 1990
RECORD CO. : GRAMAVISION/TOKUMA(JAPAN)
RECORD NO. : TKCB-30171

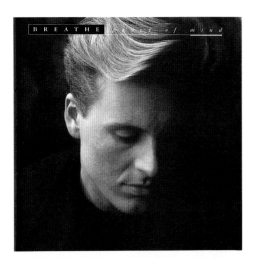
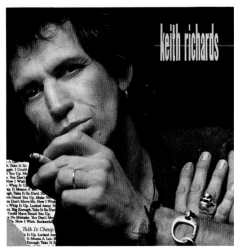
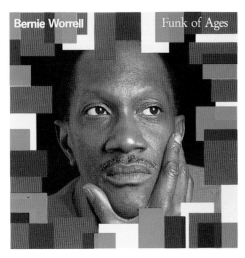
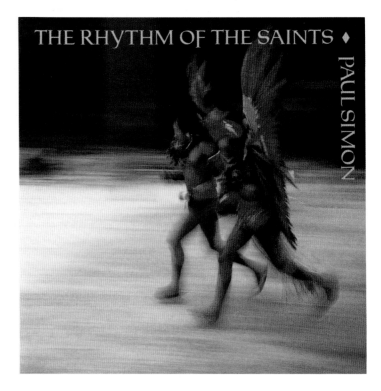
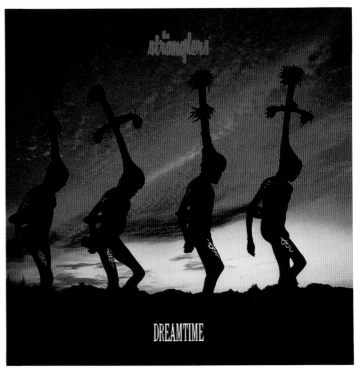

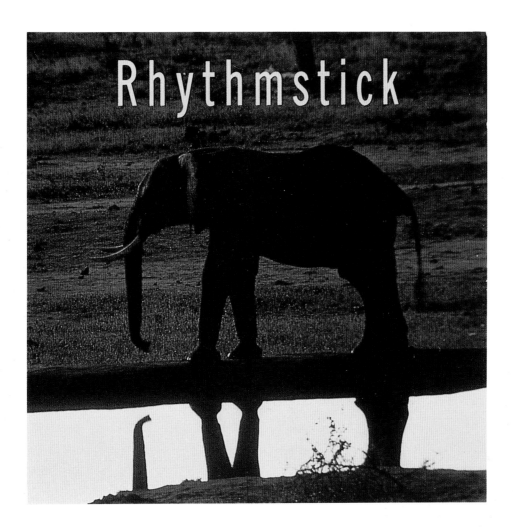

284. RHYTHMSTICK

ART DIRECTION : BLAKE TAYLOR
DESIGN : BLAKE TAYLOR
PHOTOGRAPHY : PETE TURNER
YEAR OF RELEASE : 1990
RECORD CO. : CTI/POLYDOR(JAPAN)
RECORD NO. : POCJ-1024

282. PAUL SIMON
"THE RHYTHM OF THE SAINTS"

ART DIRECTION : YOLANDA CUOMO
DESIGN : YOLANDA CUOMO
PHOTOGRAPHY : MIGUEL RIO BRANCO
YEAR OF RELEASE : 1990
RECORD CO. : WARNER
/WARNER PIONEER(JAPAN)
RECORD NO. : WPCP 3887

283. THE STRANGLERS "DREAMTIME"

DESIGN : JEAN-LUKE EPSTEIN
YEAR OF RELEASE : 1986
RECORD CO. : EPIC/EPIC SONY(JAPAN)
RECORD NO. : 32•8P-175

285. MICHAEL FRANKS "BLUE PACIFIC"
ART DIRECTION : HEIDEN/HEIDEN
DESIGN : HEIDEN/HEIDEN
PHOTOGRAPHY : KIP LOTT
YEAR OF RELEASE : 1990
RECORD CO. : REPRISE/WARNER PIONEER(JAPAN)
RECORD NO. : WPCP-3596

286. HELEN MERRILL
"HELEN MERRILL WITH CLIFFORD BROWN"
RECORD CO. : EMARCY/PHONOGRAM(JAPAN)
RECORD NO. : EJD-3001

287. "SAME OTHER TIME,
A TRIBUTE TO CHET BAKER"
YEAR OF RELEASE : 1990
RECORD CO. : ALFA(JAPAN)
RECORD NO. : ALCR-71

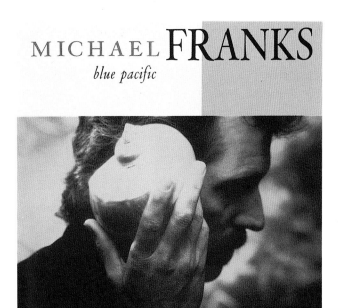

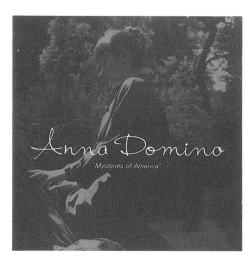

288. ANNA DOMINO
"MYSTERIES OF AMERICA"
YEAR OF RELEASE : 1990
RECORD CO. : CREPUSCULE
/VICTOR(JAPAN)
RECORD NO. : VICP-84

289. EVERYTHING BUT THE GIRL
"THE LANGUAGE OF LIFE"
DESIGN : THE SENATE
PHOTOGRAPHY : NICK KNIGHT
ILLUSTRATION : DIRK VAN DOOREN
YEAR OF RELEASE : 1990
RECORD CO. : WEA/VAP(JAPAN)
RECORD NO. : VPCK-85056

290. EDIE BRICKELL AND NEW BOHEMIANS
ART DIRECTION : EDIE BRICKELL
CREATIVE DIRECTION : ROBIN SLOANE
DESIGN : JANET WOLSBORN, LYN BRADLEY
PHOTOGRAPHY : DREW CAROLAN
YEAR OF RELEASE : 1990
RECORD CO. : GEFFEN

291. VERONIQUE RIVIERE "RIVIERE"
ART DIRECTION : HUART/CHOLLEY
DESIGN : HUART/CHOLLEY
PHOTOGRAPHY : RUSSEL YOUNG
YEAR OF RELEASE : 1989
RECORD CO. : POLYDOR

292. INDIGO GIRLS
ART DIRECTION : STEPHEN BYRAM
PHOTOGRAPHY : LENA BERTUCCI
YEAR OF RELEASE : 1989
RECORD CO. : CBS/EPIC SONY(JAPAN)
RECORD NO. : 25·8P-5275

293. THE WELLS
"THIS IS THE GUNS OF HEART"
DESIGN : SEX MIXER
PHOTOGRAPHY : ROBERT CAPA
YEAR OF RELEASE : 1989
RECORD CO. : TRANSISTER(JAPAN)
RECORD NO. : WELL-001

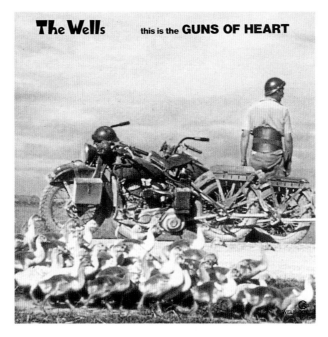

294. THE WELLS "ROUGH LABOUR"
CREATIVE DIRECTION : SHIGEO GOTO
ART DIRECTION : TSUGUYA INOUE
DESIGN : BEANS
PHOTOGRAPHY : KYOJI TAKAHASHI
YEAR OF RELEASE : 1990
RECORD CO. : COLUMBIA(JAPAN)
RECORD NO. : COCA-6848

iLLUSTRATiON

上々颱風

SHANG
SHANG
TYPHOON

295. SHANG SHANG TYPHOON

ART DIRECTION : HATUYO EGAWA
DESIGN : HATUYO EGAWA, MICIHIRO ISHIZAKI
ILLUSTRATION : JOEL A. MILLER
YEAR OF RELEASE : 1990
RECORD CO. : EPIC SONY(JAPAN)
RECORD NO. : ESCB-1090

CD Single

296. SOUL II SOUL "PEOPLE"
YEAR OF RELEASE : 1990
RECORD CO. : VIRGIN/VIRGIN(JAPAN)
RECORD NO. : VJCP-1411

297. SOUL II SOUL "1990 A NEW DANCE VOL. II"
ART DIRECTION : JAZZIE BLSIMON TAYLOR-VIVID
DESIGN : SIMON TAYLOR
PHOTOGRAPHY : NIA
ILLUSTRATION : SIMON TAYLOR
YEAR OF RELEASE : 1990
RECORD CO. : VIRGIN/VIRGIN(JAPAN)
RECORD NO. : VJCP-24

Back & Front

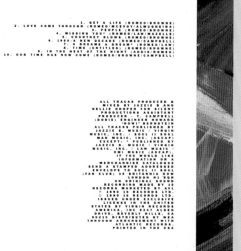

Inside spreads

298. DON PULLEN "RANDOM THOUGHTS"

ART DIRECTION : CAROL FRIEDMAN

DESIGN : PATRICK ROQUES

PHOTOGRAPHY : CAROL FRIEDMAN

ILLUSTRATION : MICHAEL J. SINGLETARY

YEAR OF RELEASE : 1990

RECORD CO. : CAPITOL/TOSHIBA EMI(JAPAN)

RECORD NO. : TOCJ-5230

299. ART ENSEMBLE OF CHICAGO SOWETO
"ART ENSEMBLE OF CHICAGO WITH AMABUTHO"

DESIGN : DIW DESIGN ROOM

PHOTOGRAPHY : HASHIMOTO

ILLUSTRATION : N.C.L AND JOE LEGUADE

YEAR OF RELEASE : 1990

RECORD CO. : DIW(JAPAN)

Recorded and mixed by Joe Marciano
Recorded and mixed at Systems Two Studios, Brooklyn, New York
December 1989 and January 1990
Cover painting by N.C.L and Joe Leguabe
Cover photos by Hashimoto/N.Y.C.
Cover design by DIW Design Room
Special thanks to Nancy Marciano, Don, Mike
and the Systems Two staff, Ameen, Larry, Kathy
and the Art Ensemble of Chicago staff.
For Promotional and/or booking information
on the Art Ensemble of Chicago
Please contact :
AECO ARTIST. Post Office Box 53429 Chicago, Illinois 60653
Attn. Ann Pryor, Phone:(312)536-2200, Fax:(312)536-2270

DIW-837

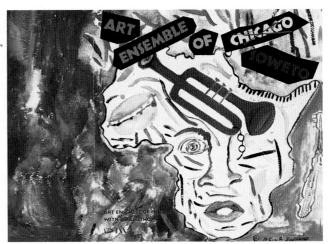

300. THE MOTELS
"THE BEST OF THE MOTELS"

ART DIRECTION : TOMMY STEELE

DESIGN : MIKE FINK

YEAR OF RELEASE : 1990

RECORD CO. : CAPITOL

301. RONALD SHANNON JACKSON AND
THE DECODING SOCIETY "MAN DANCE"

ART DIRECTION : EIKO ISHIOKA

DESIGN : EIKO ISHIOKA

PHOTOGRAPHY : DEBORAH FEINGOLD

ILLUSTRATION : KATSU YOSHIDA

YEAR OF RELEASE : 1982

RECORD CO. : ISLAND

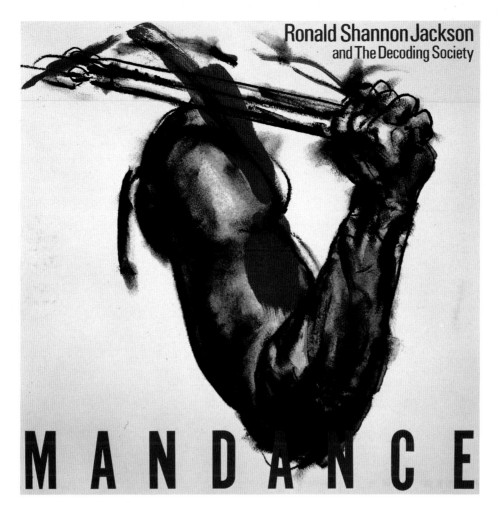

302. INDIGO GIRLS
"NOMADS · INDIANS · SAINTS"
PHOTOGRAPHY : DOROTHY GRIFFITH
ILLUSTRATION : TODD MURPHY
YEAR OF RELEASE : 1990
RECORD CO. : CBS/EPIC SONY(JAPAN)
RECORD NO. : ESCA 5177

303. UB 40 "BAGGARIDDIM"
ART DIRECTION : UB 40, BRIAN TRAVERS
DESIGN : THE DESIGN CLINIC
PHOTOGRAPHY : SIMON FOWLER
ILLUSTRATION : DAVID DRAGON
YEAR OF RELEASE : 1985
RECORD CO. : VIRGIN/VIRGIN(JAPAN)
RECORD NO. : VJD-28227

304. LOS TUPAMAROS
"SALSA Y TROPICAL"
DESIGN : MICHAEL NASH ASSOC
PHOTOGRAPHY : ADRIAN BOOT
ILLUSTRATION : ARCHER/QUINNELL
YEAR OF RELEASE : 1990
RECORD CO. : ISLAND

305. CAPPING DAY
"POST NO BILLS"
ART DIRECTION : BONNIE HAMMOND
DESIGN : BONNIE HAMMOND
ILLUSTRATION : CARL SUGARMAN
YEAR OF RELEASE : 1990
RECORD CO. : POPLLAMA

306. HAPPY MONDAYS "BUMMED"
ART DIRECTION : CENTRAL STATION DESIGN
DESIGN : CENTRAL STATION DESIGN
ILLUSTRATION : CENTRAL STATION DESIGN
YEAR OF RELEASE : 1988
RECORD CO. : FACTORY/COLUMBIA(JAPAN)
RECORD NO. : 28CY-3182

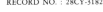

Back & Front

307. FRANK TOVEY
  "TYRANNY AND THE HIRED HAND"
DESIGN : ME COMPANY
PHOTOGRAPHY : FRANK TOVEY
ILLUSTRATION : FRANK TOVEY
YEAR OF RELEASE : 1989
RECORD CO. : MUTE

308. BOB DYLAN "OH MERCY"
ART : TROTSKY
DESIGN : CHRISTOPHER AUSTOPCHUK
PHOTOGRAPHY : SUZIE-Q
YEAR OF RELEASE : 1989
RECORD CO. : CBS/CBS SONY(JAPAN)
RECORD NO. : CSCS-5058

309. THE FATIMA MANSIONS "HIVE"
ILLUSTRATION : LAWRENCE BAGLE
YEAR OF RELEASE : 1991
RECORD CO. : KITCHENWARE

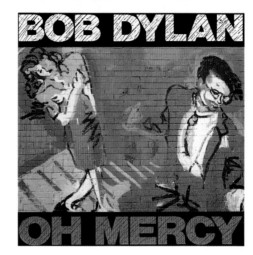

12" Single

310. SONIC YOUTH
  "CONFUSION IS SEX"
YEAR OF RELEASE : 1983
RECORD CO. : SST

311. SONIC YOUTH "SISTER"
RECORD CO. : SST

**312. JANE'S ADDICTION
"RITUAL DE LO HABITUAL"**
ART DIRECTION : PERRY FARRELL
DESIGN : TOM RECCHION
PHOTOGRAPHY : VICTOR BRACKE
SCULPTURE : PERRY AND CASEY
YEAR OF RELEASE : 1990
RECORD CO. : WARNER
/WARNER PIONEER(JAPAN)
RECORD NO. : WPCP-3711

313. THE CURE "LOVE SONG"
ART : MAYA
YEAR OF RELEASE : 1989
RECORD CO. : ELEKTRA ASYLUM

314. HIKASU "NINGEN NO KAO"
ART DIRECTION : TARO MANABE
ILLUSTRATION : TARO MANABE
YEAR OF RELEASE : 1988
RECORD CO. : PUZZLIN(JAPAN)
RECORD NO. : RWD-8

315. NEVILLE BROTHERS "BROTHER'S KEEPER"
ART DIRECTION : CHUCK BEESON, F. RON MILLER
ILLUSTRATION : ALISON SAAR
YEAR OF RELEASE : 1990
RECORD CO. : A & M/PONY CANYON(JAPAN)
RECORD NO. : PC-PCCY 10140

316. NEVILLE BROTHERS "YELLOW MOON"
ART DIRECTION : JEFF GOLD
DESIGN : MARY MAURER
ILLUSTRATION : TONY FITZPATRICK
YEAR OF RELEASE : 1989
RECORD CO. : A & M/PONY CANYON(JAPAN)
RECORD NO. : D22Y-3354

317. KING CRIMSON
  "IN THE COURT OF THE CRIMSON KING"
ILLUSTRATION : BARRY GODBER
YEAR OF RELEASE : 1969
RECORD CO. : VIRGIN/VIRGIN(JAPAN)
RECORD NO. : VJCP-2301

318. THE BIG BROTHER "L.A. TIME"
ART DIRECTION : ART & WORK-MILAN
DESIGN : SERGIO NIGRO
PHOTOGRAPHY : SERGIO NIGRO
ILLUSTRATION : SERGIO NIGRO
YEAR OF RELEASE : 1990
RECORD CO. : RODGERS AND CONTINI
/AVEX TRAX(JAPAN)

319. ROBERT STONE "BURNING HEART"
ART DIRECTION : ART & WORK-MILAN
DESIGN : SERGIO NIGRO
PHOTOGRAPHY : SERGIO NIGRO
ILLUSTRATION : SERGIO NIGRO
YEAR OF RELEASE : 1990
RECORD CO. : RODGERS AND CONTINI
/AVEX TRAX(JAPAN)

Back & Front

12" Single

12" Single

320. BAKUFU-SLUMP "ORAGAYO"
ART DIRECTION : TAKUJI NOMOTO
DESIGN : TAKUJI NOMOTO
COVER PAINTING : MARK KOSTABI
YEAR OF RELEASE : 1990
RECORD CO. : CBS SONY(JAPAN)
RECORD NO. : CSCL-1559

321. VARIOUS ARTISTS
  "ROCK AND SOUL BALLAD"
ART DIRECTION : HIDEKI YAMAZAKI
OBJECT ART : KAZUNORI KANDA
DESIGN : HIDEKI YAMAZAKI
PHOTOGRAPHY : KOH HOSOKAWA
YEAR OF RELEASE : 1990
RECORD CO. : CBS SONY(JAPAN)
RECORD NO. : CSCS-5360

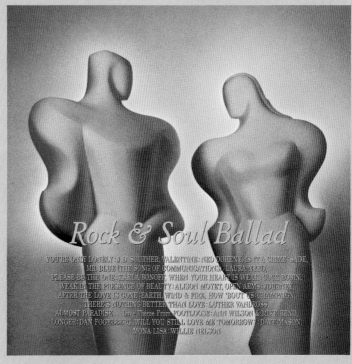

12" Single

322. THE THE "INFECTED"
ILLUSTRATION : ANDY DOG
YEAR OF RELEASE : 1986
RECORD CO. : CBS/EPIC SONY(JAPAN)
RECORD NO. : ESCA-5095

323. THE THE "SOUL MINING"
ILLUSTRATION : ANDY DOG
YEAR OF RELEASE : 1983
RECORD CO. : EPIC/EPIC SONY(JAPAN)
RECORD NO. : ES•CA-5094

**324. DREAM WARRIORS
"MY DEFINITION OF
A BOOMBASTIC JAZZ STYLE"**
TYPO DESIGN : SWIFTY
ILLUSTRATION : MR WRIGHT
RECORD CO. : ISLAND

**325. THE JAZZ BUTCHER
"CULT OF THE BASEMENT"**
PHOTOGRAPHY : ALISTAIR INDGE,
DAVID WHITTEMORE
ILLUSTRATION : PASCAL LEGRAS
YEAR OF RELEASE : 1990
RECORD CO. : CREATION/VICTOR(JAPAN)
RECORD NO. : VICP-79

**326. A TRIBE CALLED QUEST
"PEOPLES INSTINCTIVE TRAVELS AND
THE PATHS OF RHYTHM"**
ART DIRECTION : JUSTIN HERZ
DESIGN : ZOMB ART DMS
PHOTOGRAPHY : ARISTOS MARCOPOULOS
ILLUSTRATION : PAIJE HUNYADY AND
BRYANT PETERS
YEAR OF RELEASE : 1990
RECORD CO. : ZOMBA RECORDING

Back & Front

Back & Front

327. PRINCE "GRAFFITI BRIDGE"
YEAR OF RELEASE : 1990
RECORD CO. : PAISLEY PARK
/WARNER PIONEER(JAPAN)
RECORD NO. : WPCP-3640

328. PRINCE AND THE REVOLUTION
"AROUND THE WORLD IN A DAY"
DESIGN : LAURA LI PUMA
ASSEMBLY : LAURA LI PUMA
ILLUSTRATION : DOUG HENDERS
YEAR OF RELEASE : 1985
RECORD CO. : WARNER
/WARNER PIONEER(JAPAN)
RECORD NO. : 20P2-2613

329. DIE KLEINEN UND DIE BÖSEN
"DEUTSCH AMERIKANISSHE FREUNDSCHAFT"
DESIGN : R. GÖRL, F. FENSTERMACHER, S. GRANT
YEAR OF RELEASE : 1980
RECORD CO. : MUTE

330. BETTY BOO "24 HOURS"

ILLUSTRATION : GEORGE MILLER

DESIGN: DESIGNLAND

PHOTOGRAPHY : PAUL COX

YEAR OF RELEASE : 1990

RECORD CO. : RHYTHM KING

CD Single Front & Back

Front & Inside spreads

CD Single Front & Back

331. BETTY BOO "BOOMANIA"

ILLUSTRATION : GEORGE MILLER

DESIGN : DESIGNLAND

PHOTOGRAPHY : PAUL COX

YEAR OF RELEASE : 1990

RECORD CO. : RHYTHM KING

332. BETTY BOO "WHERE ARE YOU BABY?"

ILLUSTRATION : GEORGE MILLER

DESIGN : DESIGNLAND

PHOTOGRAPHY : JULIAN BARTON

YEAR OF RELEASE : 1990

RECORD CO. : RHYTHM KING

CD Single

333. SNAP "MARY HAD A LITTLE BOY"

DESIGN : ARIOLA-STUDIOS

PHOTOGRAPHY : PATRIK QUIGLY

ILLUSTRATION : TOM

YEAR OF RELEASE : 1990

RECORD CO. : ARISTA

CD Single Front & Back

334. KITCHENS OF DISTINCTION
"QUICK AS RAINBOWS"

DESIGN : ME COMPANY

YEAR OF RELEASE : 1990

RECORD CO. : ONE LITTLE INDIAN

12" Single

335. KITCHENS OF DISTINCTION
  "LOVE IS HELL"
DESIGN : ME COMPANY
YEAR OF RELEASE : 1989
RECORD CO. : ONE LITTLE INDIAN/COLUMBIA(JAPAN)
RECORD NO. : COCY-6419

336. NEW YORK HOUSE 'N AUTHORITY
DESIGN : NIGEL PROKTOR
YEAR OF RELEASE : 1990
RECORD CO. : SBK

337. BASS-O-MATIC
  "FASCINATING RHYTHM"
DESIGN : C-SOAR
YEAR OF RELEASE : 1990
RECORD CO. : VIRGIN

338. TACK-HEAD "STRANGE THINGS"
DESIGN : ME COMPANY
YEAR OF RELEASE : 1990
RECORD CO. : SBK

339. ADAMSKI "THE SPACE JUNGLE"
YEAR OF RELEASE : 1990
RECORD CO. : MCA

**340. KING KONG & THE D. JUNGLE GIRLS
"LOVE & AMERICAN DOLLARS"**
ART DIRECTION : DAGO(ELENA D'AGOSTINO)
DESIGN : DAGO
PHOTOGRAPHY : JEAN LUC DORN
ILLUSTRATION : DAGO
YEAR OF RELEASE : 1991
RECORD CO. : ALA BIANCA

12" Single

12" Single

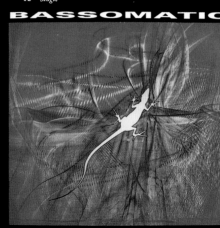

12" Single

341. BASS-O-MATIC "EASE ON BY REMIX"
ART DIRECTION : CATHERINE MCRAE
DESIGN : DAVID LITTLE
ILLUSTRATION : DAVID LITTLE
YEAR OF BELEASE : 1990
RECORD CO. : VIRGIN

342. BASS-O-MATIC "EASE ON BY"
ART DIRECTION : THE BIG BLUE
DESIGN : DAVID LITTLE
YEAR OF RELEASE : 1990
RECORD CO. : VIRGIN

12" Single

343. THE BEATMASTERS
"ANYWAYAWANNA"
DESIGN : DESIGNLAND
TYPO DESIGN : DESIGNLAND
YEAR OF RELEASE : 1990
RECORD CO. : RHYTHMKING

Inside spreads

344. P I L "THE GREATEST HITS SO FAR"
ART DIRECTION : MELANIE NISSEN
DESIGN : KATHLEEN PHILPOTT
PHOTOGRAPHY : ROSS HALFIN
ILLUSTRATION : REG MOMBASSA
YEAR OF RELEASE : 1990
RECORD CO. : VIRGIN

345. WAS(NOT WAS) "ARE YOU O.K?"
ART DIRECTION : PHONOGRAM ART
ILLUSTRATION : MARK RYDEN
PAINT BOX OPERATOR : TIM WHITELEY
YEAR OF RELEASE : 1990
RECORD CO. : CHRYSALIS

346. MORIO AGATA "MIQY OH!!"
DESIGN : KYOMITU MIHARA
ILLUSTRATION : KAZUO KAWAKAMI
RECORD CO. : COLUMBIA(JAPAN)
RECORD NO. : 32CA-2571

347. WAS(NOT WAS)
  "I FEEL BETTER THAN JAMES BROWN"
ILLUSTRATION : CHRIS LONG WITH
THE UNKNOWN PARTNERSHIP
YEAR OF RELEASE : 1990
RECORD CO. : PHONOGRAM

12" Single

348. PEARL BROTHERS "IROIKA"
ART DIRECTION : SUZY AMAKANE
ILLUSTRATION : SHIGERU SUGIURA
YEAR OF RELEASE : 1989
RECORD CO. : POLYDOR(JAPAN)
RECORD NO. : HOOP 20345

349. ROBBIN HARRIS "BÉ-BÉ'S KIDS"
ART DIRECTION : MITCHELL KANNER
DESIGN : SCOTT TOWNSEND
ILLUSTRATION : HUNGRY DOG STUDIO
YEAR OF RELEASE : 1990
RECORD CO. : POLYGRAM

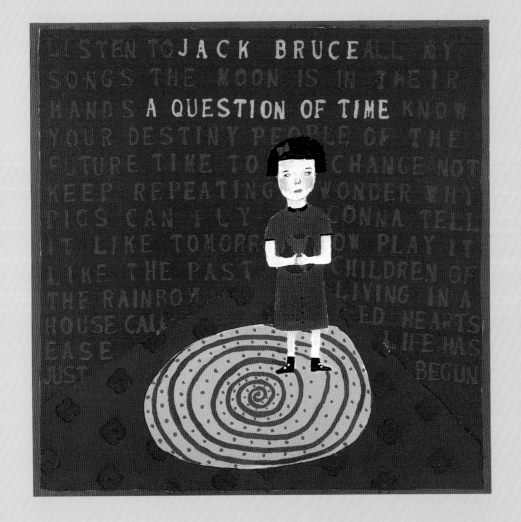

350. LADYSMITH BLACK MAMBAZO
"TWO WORLD ONE HEART"
DESIGN : STABLE GRAPHICS
ILLUSTRATION : PAUL DE CARVALHO
YEAR OF RELEASE : 1990
RECORD CO. : WARNER/WARNER PIONEER(JAPAN)
RECORD NO. : WPCP-3506

351. ZACHARY RICHARD
"ZACK'S BON TON"
ART : FRANCIS XAVIER PAVY
PHOTOGRAPHY : PHILIP GOULD
YEAR OF RELEASE : 1988
RECORD CO. : ROUNDER

352. JACK BRUCE "A QUESTION OF TIME"
ART DIRECTION : CHRIS AUSTOPCHUK
DESIGN : LAURA LEVINE
YEAR OF RELEASE : 1989
RECORD CO. : EPIC/EPIC SONY(JAPAN)
RECORD NO. : ES・CA-5024

353. VARIOUS ARTISTS
"REGGAE ATTACK"
YEAR OF RELEASE : 1990
RECORD CO. : ATTACK

354. CASABLANCA CLUB
"FEATURING LOLLY & BABY"
ILLUSTRATION : MONICA FRANCESCHI
YEAR OF RELEASE : 1990
RECORD CO. : FULL TIME

355. DANCE HALL STYLEE
"THE BEST OF REGGAE
DANCE HALL MUSIC VOL.2"
ART DIRECTION : RICK DEHAAN
DESIGN : RICK DEHAAN
ILLUSTRATION : JOSE ORTEGA
YEAR OF RELEASE : 1990
RECORD CO. : PROFILE

356. MARTIN DENNY "EXOTICA '90"
ART DIRECTION : YOSUKE KAWAMURA
PHOTOGRAPHY : PHILIP SPALDING III
ILLUSTRATION : YOSUKE KAWAMURA
YEAR OF RELEASE : 1990
RECORD CO. : TOSHIBA EMI(JAPAN)
RECORD NO. : TOCP-6160

357. ELVY SUKAESIH "PESTA PANEN"
COMPILED & CREATIVE DIRECTION : SHIZUO "EC" ISHII
ART DIRECTION : TAICH "WOO" AKASHI
ILLUSTRATION : PATER SATO
YEAR OF RELEASE : 1990
RECORD CO. : PONY CANYON(JAPAN)
RECORD NO. : PCCY-00076

358. ELVY SUKAESIH "DANGDUT TERAPIK"
CREATIVE DIRECTION : SHIZUO "EC" ISHII
ART DIRECTION : TAICHI "WOO" AKASHI
YEAR OF RELEASE : 1990
ILLUSTRATION : PATER SATO
RECORD CO. : PONY CANYON(JAPAN)
RECORD NO. : PCCY-00098

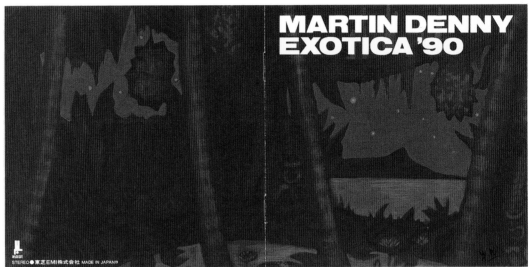

Back & Front

Back & Front

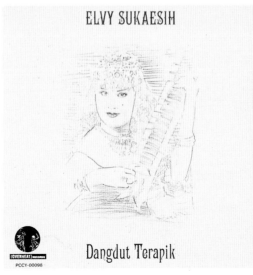

Back & Front

359. MICHIKO SHIMIZU "SHIAWASE NO KODAMA"
ART DIRECTION : MIWA HAYAKAWA
ILLUSTRATION : EMIKO SHIMODA,
MICHIKO SHIMIZU
YEAR OF RELEASE : 1989
RECORD CO. : MIDI(JAPAN)
RECORD NO. : 30MD-2511

360. MICHIKO SHIMIZU "SHIAWASE NO KOTUCHO"
DESIGN : EYE-SOME DESIGN
ILLUSTRATION : EMIKO SHIMODA
YEAR OF RELEASE : 1987
RECORD CO. : MIDI(JAPAN)
RECORD NO. : 30MD-2509

361. MICHIKO SHIMIZU "MISS VOICES"
DESIGN : MIKE SMITH(FLAMINGO STUDIO)
ILLUSTRATION : TERY JHONSON(FLAMINGO STUDIO)
YEAR OF RELEASE : 1990
RECORD CO. : MIDI(JAPAN)
RECORD NO. : MDC5-1118

Back & Front

362. THE STALIN "MUSHI"

YEAR OF RELEASE : 1989

RECORD CO. : TOKUMA(JAPAN)

RECORD NO. : 27WXD-115

363. YOSHITAKA MINAMI "BOUKENOH"

DESIGN : AKIO NINBARI

RECORD CO. : CBS SONY(JAPAN)

RECORD NO. : 32DH-745

364. KENJI ENDO "UCHU BOUEI GUN"

ART DIRECTION : KENJI ENDO

DESIGN : TATUTO SAITO, YOSHINOBU YAMAGUCHI

PHOTOGRAPHY : KENJI ENDO

ILLUSTRATION : KAZUKI MIYATAKE

YEAR OF RELEASE : 1989

RECORD CO. : KING(JAPAN)

RECORD NO. : K25X-373

365. SHONEN HOMERUNS "SHONEN HOMERUNS 12"

ART DIRECTION : TOMOHIRO ITAMI

DESIGN : IT IS DESIGN

ILLUSTRATION : KEIICHI OHTA

YEAR OF RELEASE : 1988

RECORD CO. : SOLID(JAPAN)

RECORD NO. : CDSOL-1004

366. KEIICHI OHTA "JINGAIDAIMAKYO"

ART DIRECTION : KEIICHI OHTA

YEAR OF RELEASE : 1990

RECORD CO. : ALFA(JAPAN)

RECORD NO. : ALCA-10

367. GUERNICA "KAIZO ENO YAKUDOU"

ART DIRECTION : KEIICHI OHTA

DESIGN : ABE HARUMI

PHOTOGRAPHY : HIROSE TADASHI

YEAR OF RELEASE : 1990

RECORD CO. : ALFA(JAPAN)

RECORD NO. : ALCA-4

368. IGGY POP "BRICK BY BRICK"
ART DIRECTION : MELANIE NISSEN
DESIGN : STEVE J. GERDES
ILLUSTRATION : CHARLES BURNS
YEAR OF RELEASE : 1990
RECORD CO. : VIRGIN/VIRGIN(JAPAN)
RECORD NO. : VJCP-39

**369. IGGY POP AND
JAMES WILLIAMSON "KILL CITY"**
DESIGN : DAVID ALLEN
YEAR OF RELEASE : 1990
RECORD CO. : LINE

370. SHIGERU IZUMIYA "ELEVATOR"
ART DIRECTION : KATSUMI ASABA
DESIGN : MASAMI YAMAMOTO
ILLUSTRATION : MASAMI YAMAMOTO
YEAR OF RELEASE : 1985
RECORD CO. : POLYDOR(JAPAN)
RECORD NO. : H32P-20239

Back & Front

371. KAN MIKAMI "BANG!"
DESIGN : TOSHIO SAEKI, TOSHIO SAKAI
RECORD CO. : KITTY(JAPAN)
RECORD NO. : H20K-25029

372. WHAT IF
ART DIRECTION : NORMAN MOORE
DESIGN : NORMAN MOORE
ILLUSTRATION : NORMAN MOORE
YEAR OF RELEASE : 1987
RECORD CO. : RCA

373. HEART "BAD ANIMALS"
ART DIRECTION : NORMAN MOORE
DESIGN : NORMAN MOORE
ILLUSTRATION : NORMAN MOORE
YEAR OF RELEASE : 1987
RECORD CO. : CAPITOL/TOSHIBA EMI(JAPAN)
RECORD NO. : CP32-5399

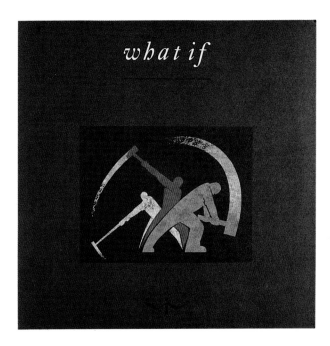

374. MAZE "THE GREATEST HITS OF MAZE"
ART DIRECTION : TOMMY STEELE
DESIGN : GLENN SAKAMOTO
ILLUSTRATION : MARK RYDEN
YEAR OF RELEASE : 1989
RECORD CO. : CAPITOL

375. PATRICK O'HEARN "ELDORADO"
ART DIRECTION : NORMAN MOORE
DESIGN : NORMAN MOORE
ILLUSTRATION : NANCY NIMOY
YEAR OF RELEASE : 1989
RECORD CO. : PRIVATE MUSIC/BMG VICTOR(JAPAN)
RECORD NO. : R32P-1244

376. TOOTS AND THE MAYTALS
"REGGAE GREATS"
ILLUSTRATION : CHRISTOPHER BROWN
YEAR OF RELEASE : 1985
RECORD CO. : ISLAND

377. PIGBAG "THE BEST OF PIGBAG"
YEAR OF RELEASE : 1987
RECORD CO. : KAZ

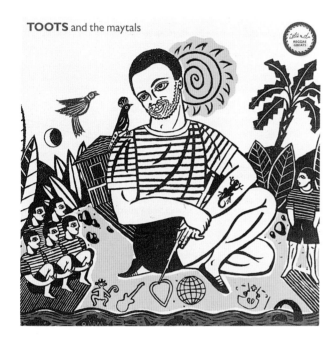

378. MICKEY HART "AT THE EDGE"
ART DIRECTION : HOWARD JACOBSEN/TRIAL
DESIGN : STEVEN JURGENSMEYER
ILLUSTRATION : NANCY NIMOY
YEAR OF RELEASE : 1990
RECORD CO. : RYKODISC

379. SINGING IN AN OPEN SPACE
"ZULU RHYTHM AND HARMONY, 1962-1982"
DESIGN : JEAN WILCOX
PHOTOGRAPHY : PAUL WEINBERG
YEAR OF RELEASE : 1990
RECORD CO. : ROUNDER

380. TATSUYA TAKAHASHI & TOKYO UNION
"PLAYS MILES & GIL"
ART DIRECTION : SHIGO YAMAGUCHI
DESIGN : SHIGO DESIGN ROOM
ILLUSTRATION : HIROSUKE UENO
YEAR OF RELEASE : 1988
RECORD CO. : KING(JAPAN)
RECORD NO. : K32Y-6268

381. MASAYUKI SUZUKI "MOOD"
ART DIRECTION : NOBUAKI TAKAHASHI
DESIGN : NOBUAKI TAKAHASHI
YEAR OF RELEASE : 1990
RECORD CO. : EPIC SONY(JAPAN)
RECORD NO. : ESCB 1094

382. YOSHIAKI OCHI "NATURAL SONIC"
ART DIRECTION : TOMOHIRO ITAMI
ILLUSTRATION : YOSHIAKI OCHI
YEAR OF RELEASE : 1990
RECORD CO. : SPIRAL(JAPAN)
RECORD NO. : 28CD-N009

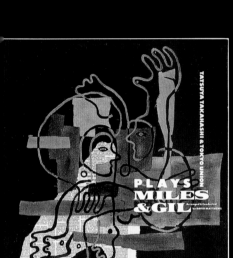

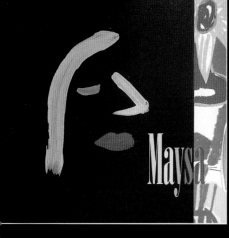

Maysa

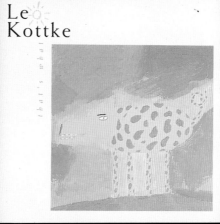

Leo Kottke
that's what

EGBERTO GISMONTI
DANÇA DOS ESCRAVOS

ECM

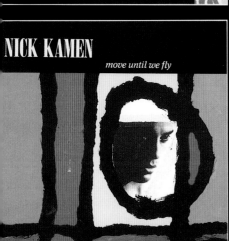

NICK KAMEN
move until we fly

LFA-1059

Cedar Walton Trio
at Good Day's club

Antonio Carlos
Jobim

392. D·O·A "MURDER"
DESIGN : RUDY TUESDAY
YEAR OF RELEASE : 1990
RECORD CO. : RESTLESS/PONY CANYON(JAPAN)
RECORD NO. : PCCY-00121

393. THE WONDER STUFF
"THE EIGHT LEGGED GROOVE MACHINE"
DESIGN : HAZEL
YEAR OF RELEASE : 1988
RECORD CO. : POLYDOR/POLYDOR(JAPAN)
RECORD NO. : POOP-20262

394. JACKSON BROWNE "LIVES IN THE BALANCE"
ART DIRECTION : JIMMY WACHTEL, DAWN PATROL
ART : RICHARD DUARDO
RECORD CO. : ELEKTRA ASYLUM
/WEA(JAPAN)
RECORD NO. : 32XD-393

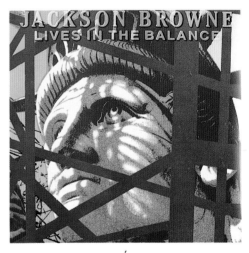

395. INSPIRAL CARPETS "ISLAND HEAD LIVE"
DESIGN : DESIGNLAND
PHOTOGRAPHY : PETER ASHWORTH
YEAR OF RELEASE : 1990
RECORD CO. : MUTE

396. IAN HUNTER "SHADES OF IAN HUNTER"
ART DIRECTION : MARC COZZA
DESIGN : MARC COZZA
ILLUSTRATION : HUBERT KRETZSCHMAR
YEAR OF RELEASE : 1988
RECORD CO. : CHRYSALIS

12" Single

397. S-KEN "MATO"

YEAR OF RELEASE : 1990
RECORD CO. : COLUMBIA(JAPAN)
RECORD NO. : COCA-6893

398. JONI MITCHELL "DOG EAT DOG"

ART DIRECTION : GLEN CHRISTENSEN
DESIGN : JONI MITCHELL
PHOTOGRAPHY : NORMAN SEEFF
ILLUSTRATION : JONI MITCHELL
YEAR OF RELEASE : 1985
RECORD CO. : GEFFEN

399. JANET JACKSON "CONTROL"

ART DIRECTION : CHUCK BEESON, MELANIE NISSEN
DESIGN : MELANIE NISSEN
PHOTOGRAPHY : TONY VIRAMONTES
YEAR OF RELEASE : 1986
RECORD CO. : A & M/PONY CANYON(JAPAN)
RECORD NO. : D22Y-3359

400. OHSHIMA NAGISA

ART DIRECTION : OHSHIMA NAGISA
DESIGN : HAJIME ANZAI
PHOTOGRAPHY : JUNSUKE TAKIMOTO
YEAR OF RELEASE : 1989
RECORD CO. : EXPLOSION WORKS(JAPAN)
RECORD NO. : ING-201065

401. FOREIGN AFFAIR "EAST ON FIRE"

DESIGN : SIGNES PARTICULIERS
PICTURES : DANNY WILLEMS
RECORD CO. : CRAMMED DISCS/TOKUMA(JAPAN)
RECORD NO. : TKCB-30060

402. GOM JABBAR DC AND PUPPA LESLIE "BELLE EPOQUE !"

ART DIRECTION : GOM JABBAR ART CLUB
PHOTOGRAPHY : DOCTOR DAMIEN
YEAR OF RELEASE : 1990
RECORD CO. : MUSIDISC/POUPEE PAT

403. RAMSA "CARTE DE SÉJOUR"

DESIGN : CORNELA CLAUSSEN
RECORD CO. : BARCLAY

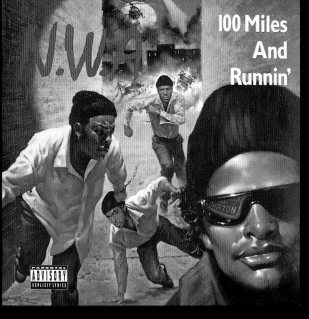

406. TALKIN LOUD

DESIGN : SWIFFY

ILLUSTRATION : WRIGHTY BOY

YEAR OF RELEASE : 1990

RECORD CO. : PHONOGRAM

/PHONOGRAM(JAPAN)

407. VARIOUS ARTISTS "BUST A RUP"

YEAR OF RELEASE : 1990

RECORD CO. : PRIORITY

408. LITTLE WILLIE JOHN "SURE THINGS"
YEAR OF RELEASE : 1990
RECORD CO. : KING/AMERICANA(JAPAN)
RECORD NO. : KCD-739

409. LIGHTNIN' HOPKINS "MOJO HAND"
RECORD CO. : P-VINE(JAPAN)
RECORD NO. : PCD-1252

410. SAM & DAVE "HOLD ON, I'M COMIN'"
ART DIRECTION : JIM STEWART
DESIGN : RONNIE STOOTS
YEAR OF RELEASE : 1966
RECORD CO. : ATLANTIC/MMG(JAPAN)
RECORD NO. : 20P2-2366

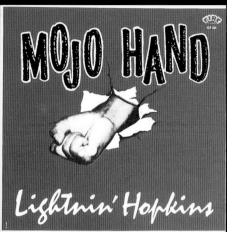
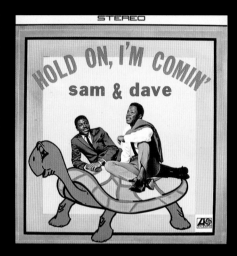

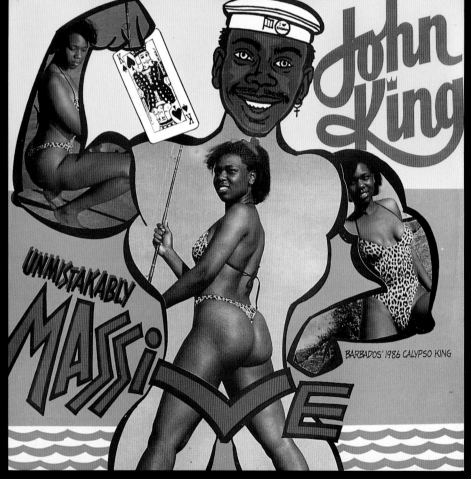

411. THE SUPER SUPER BLUES BAND
"FEATURING MUDDY WATERS,
HOWLIN' WOLF BO DIDDLEY, LITTLE WALTER"
DESIGN : ATSUO HAYAKAWA
RECORD CO. : P-VINE(JAPAN)
RECORD NO. : PLP-6075

413. JOHN KING "UNMISTAKABLY MASSIVE"
DESIGN : WINSTON JORDAN
PHOTOGRAPHY : ERROL NURSE
YEAR OF RELEASE : 1989
RECORD CO. : J & K MUSIC

414. RYUDOGUMI
"TOKYO BLOOD SWEAT AND TEARS"
ART DIRECTION : NOBUAKI TAKAHASHI
DESIGN : NOBUAKI TAKAHASHI
YEAR OF RELEASE : 1990
RECORD CO. : EPIC SONY(JAPAN)
RECORD NO. : ESCB 1119

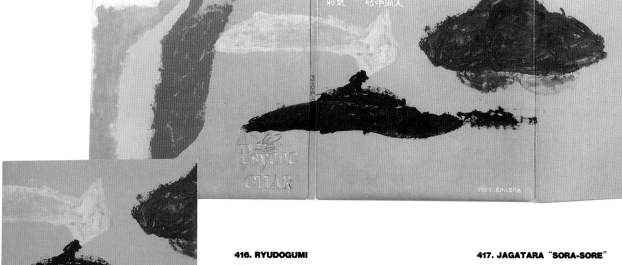

415. CHAR "PSYCHE"
ART DIRECTION : CHAR
DESIGN : WHITH ART
ILLUSTRATION : JESSE MC FADDIN
YEAR OF RELEASE : 1988
RECORD CO. : EDOYA(JAPAN)
RECORD NO. : PSY-1

416. RYUDOGUMI
ART DIRECTION : YASUTAKA KATO
PHOTOGRAPHY : SHIGERU BANDO
ILLUSTRATION : HIDEO IGAWA
YEAR OF RELEASE : 1985
RECORD CO. : CBS SONY(JAPAN)
RECORD NO. : 40·8H-58

417. JAGATARA "SORA-SORE"
ART DIRECTION : YASUO YAGI FOR PICTOX 72
DESIGN : PICTOX
PHOTOGRAPHY : SACHIO ONO
ILLUSTRATION : KAZUFUMI KODAMA
YEAR OF RELEASE : 1990
RECORD CO. : BMG VICTOR(JAPAN)
RECORD NO. : BVCR-9001

Back & Front

Back & Front

418. RINKENBAND "NANKURU"
DESIGN : SAMURAI
YEAR OF RELEASE : 1990
RECORD CO. : WAVE(JAPAN)
RECORD NO. : EVA-4004

419. X "BLUE BLOOD"
CREATIVE DIRECTION : SHIGEO GOTO
ART DIRECTION : MASAYOSHI NAKAJO
DESIGN : MASAYOSHI NAKAJO
YEAR OF RELEASE : 1989
RECORD CO. : CBS SONY(JAPAN)
RECORD NO. : 32DH 5224

420. ANGIE "MADO NO KUCIBUEFUKI"

ART DIRECTION : TADASHI SHIMADA

DESIGN : TADASHI SHIMADA, SHIGEKI YAMANAKA

ILLUSTRATION : SHINYA FUKAZU

YEAR OF RELEASE : 1990

RECORD CO. : MELDAC(JAPAN)

RECORD NO. : MECR-28010

421. SADISTIC MICA BAND "APPARE"

ART DIRECTION : YUKIMASA OKUMURA

DESIGN : MITSUNOBU MURAKAMI

PHOTOGRAPHY : KENJI MIURA

YEAR OF RELEASE : 1989

RECORD CO. : TOSHIBA EMI(JAPAN)

RECORD NO. : CT32-5432

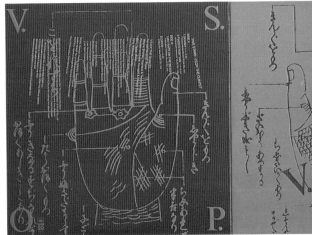

Back & Front

422. V.S.O.P. THE QUINTET "FIVE STARS"

ART DIRECTION : EIKO ISHIOKA

DESIGN : EIKO ISHIOKA, MOTOKO NARUSE

YEAR OF RELEASE : 1979

RECORD CO. : CBS SONY(JAPAN)

RECORD NO. : 40DP-5610～1

Back   *Front*

423. MASAHIKO SATOH "ALL-IN ALL-OUT"

ART DIRECTION : EIKO ISHIOKA

DESIGN : EIKO ISHIOKA, MOTOKO NARUSE

YEAR OF RELEASE : 1979

RECORD CO. : CBS SONY(JAPAN)

424. KITARO "KOJIKI"
ART DIRECTION : GOOFY MORI
DESIGN : MASAKAZU HIRAO
ILLUSTRATION : MIYUKI UEDA
YEAR OF RELEASE : 1990
RECORD CO. : GEFFEN
/MCA VICTOR(JAPAN)
RECORD NO. : NVCG-52

425. MICHAEL LANDAU
"TALES FROM THE BULGE"
ART DIRECTION : YOHKO HAMADA
DESIGN : YOHKO HAMADA
ILLUSTRATION : YASUHIRO SAWADA
YEAR OF RELEASE : 1990
RECORD CO. : SOHBI(JAPAN)
RECORD NO. : SFB-1004

426. PIETER NOOTEN, MICHAEL BROOK
ART DIRECTION : VAUGHAN OLIVER
DESIGN : VAUGHAN OLIVER
CALLIGRAPHY : CHRISTOPHER BIGG
YEAR OF RELEASE : 1987
RECORD CO. : 4AD/COLUMBIA(JAPAN)
RECORD NO. : 33CY-2084

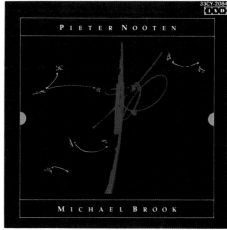

427. THE CURE "CLOSE TO ME"
RECORD CO. : ELEKTRA

428. PRISM "MOTHER EARTH"
ART DIRECTION : MAKOTO CHINEN
DESIGN : MAKOTO CHINEN
ILLUSTRATION : SHINGO FUNAZAWA
YEAR OF RELEASE : 1990
RECORD CO. : BANDAI(JAPAN)
RECORD NO. : BCCY-2

429. KENJI ENDO "KENJI"
DESIGN : OSAMU SAKAI
ART : TADANORI YOKOO
YEAR OF RELEASE : 1974
RECORD CO. : POLYDOR(JAPAN)
RECORD NO. : HOOP-20335

430. SHOUKICHI KINA "CELEBRATION"
DESIGN : HAJIME ANZAI, NOBORU SUZUKI, MR. OGURA
ILLUSTRATION : SHOUKICHI KINA
YEAR OF RELEASE : 1990
RECORD CO. : VAP(JAPAN)
RECORD NO. : VPCC-83003

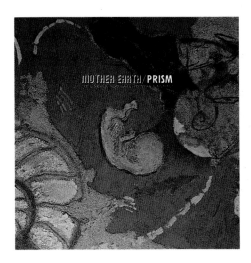

Back & Front

431. VARIOUS ARTISTS "TRANS CRAZE"
ART DIRECTION : KAZUNORI AKITA
DESIGN : KAZUNORI AKITA
RECORD CO. : INNER DIRECTS(JAPAN)
RECORD NO. : WCD-10

432. TAEKO ONUKI "NEW MOON"
ART DIRECTION : KOHICHI YOSHIDA
PHOTOGRAPHY : KENJI TOHMA
ILLUSTRATION : KENJI TOHMA
YEAR OF RELEASE : 1990
RECORD CO. : MIDI(JAPAN)
RECORD NO. : 32MD-1068

433. MAE MCKENNA "NIGHTFALLERS"
ART DIRECTION : CATHERINE MCRAE/DECLAN COLGAN
DESIGN : ANDREN ELLIS/ICON DESIGN
ILLUSTRATION : ANDREIW ELLIS
YEAR OF RELEASE : 1990
RECORD CO. : VIRGIN/VIRGIN(JAPAN)
RECORD NO. : VJCP-4

434. FETCHIN BONES "MONSTER"
ART DIRECTION : TOMMY STEELE
ILLUSTRATION : MARK RYDEN
YEAR OF RELEASE : 1989
RECORD CO. : CAPITOL

435. CRIME AND THE CITY SOLUTIONS
    "PARADISE DISCOTHEQUE"
ART WORK : A. HACKE
DESIGN : DESIGNLAND
YEAR OF RELEASE : 1990
RECORD CO. : MUTE/ALFA(JAPAN)
RECORD NO. : ALCB-127

12″ Single

436. TALK TALK "LIFE'S WHAT YOU MAKE IT"
DESIGN : PEACOCK MARKETING & DESIGN
ILLUSTRATION : JAMES MARSH
YEAR OF RELEASE : 1990
RECORD CO. : EMI

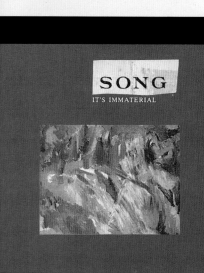

443. THE BOLSHOI "LINDY'S PARTY"
DESIGN : JAN KALICKI
PHOTOGRAPHY : PAUL COX
ILLUSTRATION : VIV MABOON
YEAR OF RELEASE : 1987
RECORD CO. : BEGGARS BANQUET

444. DEAD CAN DANCE "AION"
ART : BRENDAN PERRY
YEAR OF RELEASE : 1990
RECORD CO. : 4AD/COLUMBIA(JAPAN)
RECORD NO. : COCY-6871

445. MORIO AGATA "LES MISERABLE"
DESIGN : HEIKICHI HARADA
PHOTOGRAPHY : AKIRA KAI, SATOSHI TAKEI
YEAR OF RELEASE : 1974
RECORD CO. : KING(JAPAN)
RECORD NO. : KICS-2012

446. THE SNAPDRAGONS
"THE ETERNAL IN A MOMENT"
ART DIRECTION : IAN ANDERSON
DESIGN : DESIGNERS REPUBLIC
YEAR OF RELEASE : 1990
RECORD CO. : NATIVE

447. VARIOUS ARTISTS
"A TRIBUTE TO THE VELVET UNDERGROUND
HEAVEN AND HELL VOL.1"
ILLUSTRATION : JEMMA LOUISE DUFFY
YEAR OF RELEASE : 1990
RECORD CO. : IMAGINARY

448. VARIOUS ARTISTS
"A TRIBUTE TO THE VELVET UNDERGROUND
HEAVEN AND HELL VOL.2"
DESIGN : STEVE HALL
ILLUSTRATION : JASON
YEAR OF RELEASE : 1990
RECORD CO. : IMAGINALY

449. ART BEARS
"WINTER SONGS THE WORLD AS IT IS TODAY"
ART : EM THOMAS
RECORD CO. : ARCADES MUSIC

450. PASCAL COMELADE "33 BARS"
DESIGN : JOSÉ GARCIA
ILLUSTRATION : LAURENT ROCHE
YEAR OF RELEASE : 1989
RECORD CO. : WAVE(JAPAN)
RECORD NO. : EVA 2011

451. SNUFF "WORKERS PLAYTIME"
YEAR OF RELEASE : 1989
RECORD CO. : WORKERS PLAYTIME

452. MICHAEL NYMAN
"DROWNING BY NUMBERS"
DESIGN : ASSORTED IMAGES & ICON
ILLUSTRATION : NUMBERS BV AN
ALLARTS PRODUCTION
RECORD CO. : VIRGIN

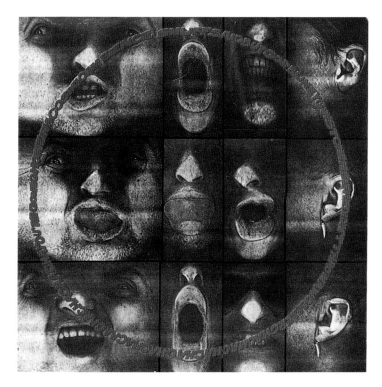

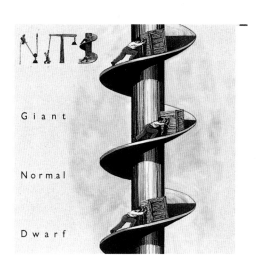

453. ZNR "TRAITÉ DE MÉCANIQUE POPULAIRE"
ART DIRECTION : GIRA-LOUIZE ALCAZAR
YEAR OF RELEASE : 1990
RECORD CO. : BUDA

454. MICHEAL PENN "MARCH"
ART DIRECTION : RIA LEWERKE
DESIGN : RIA LEWERKE
PHOTOGRAPHY : GLENN URLER
ILLUSTRATION : DAVID SHANNON.
YEAR OF RELEASE : 1990
RECORD CO. : RCA/BMG VICTOR(JAPAN)
RECORD NO. : BVCP-2501

455. THE NITS "GIANT NORMAL DWARF"
DESIGN : RIEMKE KUIPERS, HENK HOFSTEDE
ILLUSTRATION : RIEMKE KUIPERS, HENK HOFSTEPE
YEAR OF RELEASE : 1990
RECORD CO. : CBS

456. THE JIMI HENDRIX EXPERIENCE
"AXIS BOLD AS LOVE"
YEAR OF RELEASE : 1967
RECORD CO. : POLYDOR/POLYDOR(JAPAN)
RECORD NO. : P20P 22002

Typography

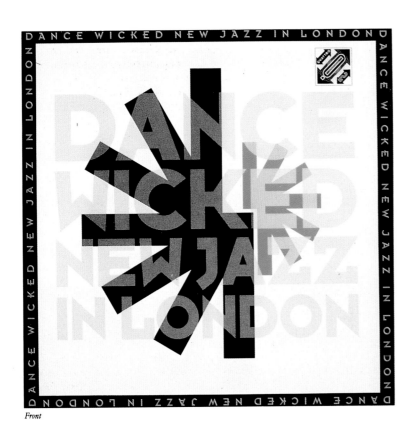

Front

457. DANCE WICKED "NEW JAZZ IN LONDON"
ART DIRECTION : NEVILLE BRODY, NANA SHIOMI
YEAR OF RELEASE : 1990
RECORD CO. : QUATTRO(JAPAN)
RECORD NO. : QTCY-2001

**458. KIRSTY MACCOLL AND THE POGUES
/AZTIC CAMERA "RED + HOT BLUE"**
DESIGN : CHRYSALIS ART "MISS OTIS"
YEAR OF RELEASE : 1990
RECORD CO. : CHRYSALIS

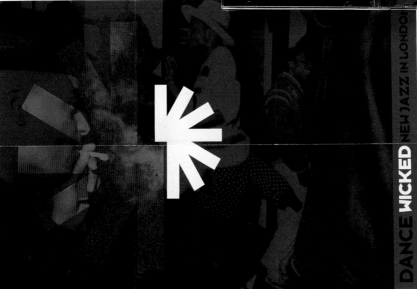

Inside spreads

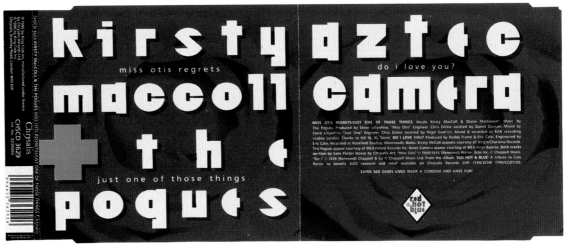

Front & Back

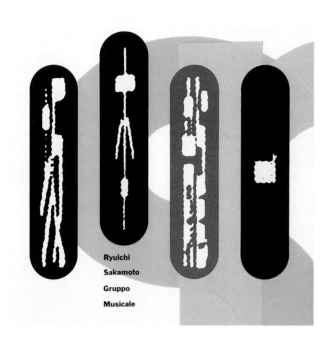

Ryuichi
Sakamoto
Gruppo
Musicale

Produced, Composed, Arranged and Performed by Ryuichi Sakamoto

459. RYUICHI SAKAMOTO "GRUPPO MUSICALE"
DESIGN : NEVILLE BRODY, TONY COOPER,
CORNEL WINDLIN,MASAYUKI TAKAHASHI
YEAR OF RELEASE : 1989
RECORD CO. : MIDI(JAPAN)
RECORD NO. : 32MD-1046

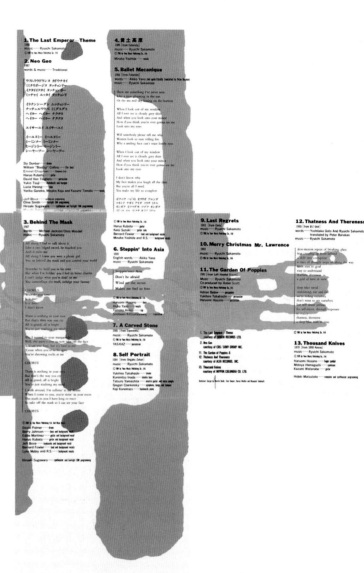

460. THE ESCAPE CLUB "DOLLARS & SEX"
DESIGN : MRGO CHASE
PHOTOGRAPHY : DAVID PROVOST
YEAR OF RELEASE : 1991
RECORD CO. : ATLANTIC

461. FINITRIBE "GROSSING 10K"
YEAR OF RELEASE : 1989
RECORD CO. : ONE LITTLE INDIAN/COLUMBIA(JAPAN)
RECORD NO. : COCY-6570

462. FYC "THE RAW & THE REMIX"
ART DIRECTION : FYC
YEAR OF RELEASE : 1990
RECORD CO. : FFRR

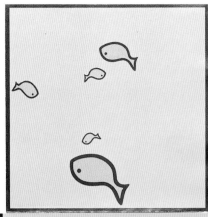

Front

1. SHE DRIVES ME CRAZY – DAVID Z
12' VERSION 2/ I'M NOT SATISFIED –
NEW YORK RAP VERSION 3/ GOOD
THING – 12' VERSION 4/ JOHNNY
COME HOME – THE MIX WITH NO BEARD
5/ I'M NOT THE MAN I USED TO BE –
JAZZIE B & NELLEE HOOPER VERSION
6/ SHE DRIVES ME CRAZY – THE MONIE
LOVE REMIX 7/ I'M NOT SATISFIED –
MATT DIKE REMIX 8/ IT'S OK (IT'S
ALRIGHT) – PLOEG CLUB MIX 9/ I'M
NOT THE MAN I USED TO BE – SMITH &
MIGHTY VERSION 10/ JOHNNY TAKES
A TRIP 71. TIRED OF GETTING
PUSHED AROUND – THE MAYHEM RHYTHM
REMIX " 12/ DON'T LOOK BACK –
12' VERSION " " " BONUS TRACKS
AVAILABLE ON CASSETTE AND CD ONLY

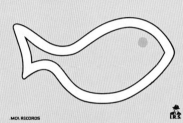

MCA RECORDS
1990 FFRR Records, Ltd. All Songs © 1990, 1989, 1988, 1987 FFRR Records, Ltd. except
"Good Thing"–12' Version" © 1989 Touchstone Pictures, and "Johnny Come Home–The
Mix With No Beard" and "Johnny Takes a Trip" © 1990 International Record Syndicate, Inc.
Manufactured and Distributed by MCA Records Inc., 70 Universal City Plaza, Universal City,
CA 91608–U.S.A. WARNING: All rights reserved. Unauthorized duplication is a violation of
applicable laws. © MCAD-10125

463. FYC "GOOD THING"
SLEEVE : MARTIN JENKINS
YEAR OF RELEASE : 1989
RECORD CO. : LONDON

Front & Back

(A) GOOD THING (7" MIX) (B) GOOD THING (NOTHING
LIKE THE SINGLE MIX) (C) SHE DRIVES ME CRAZY
(MONIE LOVE REMIX) (D) SOCIAL SECURITY. (A) (B)
(D) PRODUCED BY COX/STEELE/GIFT (C) BY DAVID Z &
FYC. REMIXED BY STEELE/COX (A 2 MEN PRODUCTION).
'GOOD THING' IS TAKEN FROM THE LP / CD /
CASSETTE 'THE RAW & THE COOKED'
ALSO FEATURING 'SHE DRIVES ME CRAZY.'
(A) (D) · 1987 TOUCHSTONE PICTURES (B) · 1989
TOUCHSTONE PICTURES (C) · 1988 FFRR RECORDS LTD.
TRADING AS LONDON RECORDS · 1989 FFRR RECORDS
LTD. TRADING AS LONDON RECORDS. SLEEVE DESIGNED
BY MARTIN JENKINS AT DKB ■ ■ ■ ■ ■ ■ ■ ■ ■

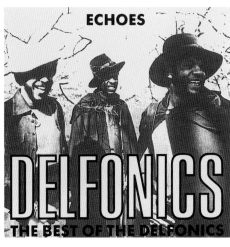

464. THEY MIGHT BE GIANTS "FLOOD"

DESIGN : HELENE SILVERMAN

PHOTOGRAPHY : MARGARET BOURKEWHITE

YEAR OF RELEASE : 1990

RECORD CO. : ELEKTRA/WEA(JAPAN)

RECORD NO. : WPCP-3435

Front & Inside spreads

465. DELFONICS "ECHOES"

YEAR OF RELEASE : 1990

RECORD CO. : BMG

466. R.E.M. "EPONYMOUS"
ART DIRECTION : RON SCARSELLI
PHOTOGRAPHY : KENNETH GARRETT
YEAR OF RELEASE : 1988
RECORD CO. : I.R.S./VICTOR(JAPAN)
RECORD NO. : VDP-1426

467. R.E.M "OUT OF TIME"
ART DIRECTION : TOM RECCHION, MICHAEL STIPE
DESIGN : TOM RECCHION, MICHAEL STIPE
YEAR OF RELEASE : 1991
RECORD CO. : WARNER/WARNER-PIONEER(JAPAN)
RECORD NO. : WPCP-4195

468. CABARET VOLTAIRE

"3 CRÉPUSCULE TRACKS"

DESIGN : NEVILLE BRODY

YEAR OF RELEASE : 1981

RECORD CO. : BRUITS ESSENTIELS

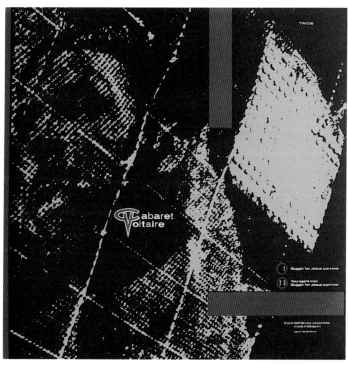

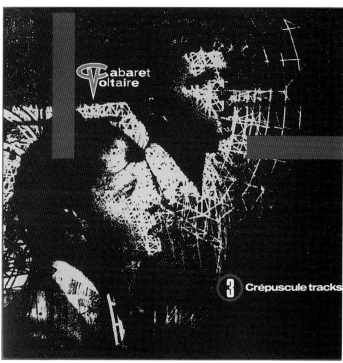

Back   *Front*

469. JAMES "HOW WAS IT FOR YOU?"

DESIGN : CHRISTOPHER LORD

YEAR OF RELEASE : 1990

RECORD CO. : FONTANA

470. JAMES "HOW WAS IT FOR YOU?"

DESIGN : CHRISTOPHER LORD

YEAR OF RELEASE : 1990

RECORD CO. : FONTANA

12″ Single   *12″ Single*

The Basement Boys
present

Ultra
Naté

Specially-Priced Maxi-Single

Is it love?

12″ Single

Side A
One—Reach out, club version (6:35)† • Two—Reach out, radio edit (3:58)† • Three—Reach out, dub (5:48)†
Side B
Four—Reach out, character mix (6:00) • Five—Reach out, character radio version (3:54) • Six—Reach out, character radio edit (3:55)

Written by Tror Taylor and Charles Farrar
Published by EMI April Music, Inc. (ASCAP)/Mamamia Music (ASCAP)/E Bam Music (ASCAP)
Produced by The Basement (Tror Taylor and Charles Farrar)
Mixed by The Chairman (except † Mixed by Tony Humphries)
Engineered by Mark Parris
Executive producer—Bob Coulomb

SBK • ONE

12″ Single Back

ELEANOR JOHNSON
•
Reach out

Stance, Trance & Dance   Dance, Trance & Stance

SBK • ONE

12″ Single Front

473. THE SUGARCUBES "DEUS"

DESIGN : P. WHITE

YEAR OF RELEASE : 1988

RECORD CO. : ONE LITTLE INDIAN

474. VARIOUS ARTISTS
"SOLID SOUNDS HARDCORE HYPNOTIC DANCE"

COVER : BITE IT!

RECORD CO. : CHAMPION

12" Single

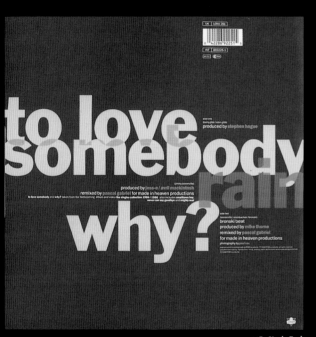

12" Single Back

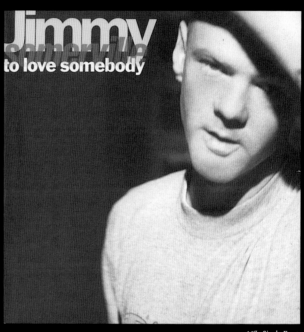

12" Single Front

475. JIMMY SOMERVILLE
"TO LOVE SOMEBODY"

PHOTOGRAPHY : PAUL COX

YEAR OF RELEASE : 1990

RECORD CO. : FFRR

476. ECHO & THE BUNNYMEN "REVERBERATION"

ART DIRECTION : ME COMPANY

DESIGN : ME COMPANY

PHOTOGRAPHY : MICHAEL MCKENZE, ADRIAN GREEN

YEAR OF RELEASE : 1990

RECORD CO. : SIRE/WEA(JAPAN)

RECORD NO. : WMC5-252

Front & Inside spreads

477. 808 STATE "EX : EL"

ART DIRECTION : TREVOR JOHNSON

DESIGN : JOHNSON PANAS

YEAR OF RELEASE : 1991

RECORD CO. : ZTT/WEA(JAPAN)

RECORD NO. : WMC5-316

478. THE DURUTTI COLUMN "OBEY THE TIME"

ART DIRECTION : 8VO

DESIGN : 8VO

YEAR OF RELEASE : 1990

RECORD CO. : FACTORY /COLUMBIA(JAPAN)

RECORD NO. : COCY-7185

479. 808 STATE "808 UTD STATE 90"

ART DIRECTION : SIMON RYAN

DESIGN : RYAN ART

ILLUSTRATION : SIMON RYAN

YEAR OF RELEASE : 1991

RECORD CO. : ZTT/WEA(JAPAN)

RECORD NO. : WMC5-50

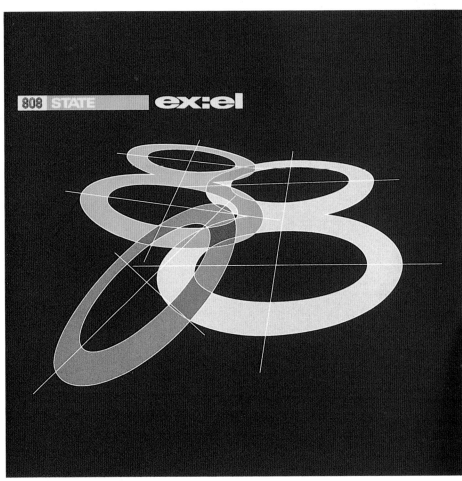

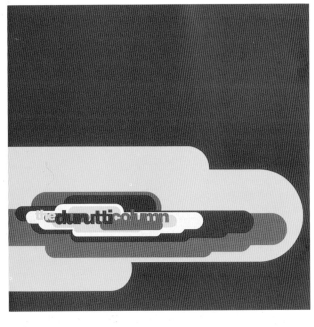

480. BANDERAS "THIS IS YOUR LIFE
/IT'S WRITTEN ALL OVER MY FACE"
ART DIRECTION : "TWO"
PHOTOGRAPHY : XAVIER GUARDAINS, DARIUS ARMSTRONG
YEAR OF RELEASE : 1991
RECORD CO. : FFRR

12" Single Back

12" Single Front

12" Single

483. CARON WHEELER "UK BLACK"
DESIGN : STEPHANIE & ANTHONY
PHOTOGRAPHY : ANDREW McPHERSON
YEAR OF RELEASE : 1990
RECORD CO. : RCA/BMG VICTOR(JAPAN)
RECORD NO. : BVCP-22

484. CARON WHEELER "UK BLACK"
PHOTOGRAPHY : ANDREW McPHERSON
YEAR OF RELEASE : 1990
RECORD CO. : RCA/BMG VICTOR(JAPAN)
RECORD NO. : BVDP-30

485. ICHIKO HASHIMOTO "JE M'AIME"
ART DIRECTION : AKIHIRO YASUDA
DESIGN : AKIHIRO YASUDA
PHOTOGRAPHY : BRUNO DAYAN
YEAR OF RELEASE : 1990
RECORD CO. : POLYDOR(JAPAN)
RECORD NO. : POCH-1004

CD Single

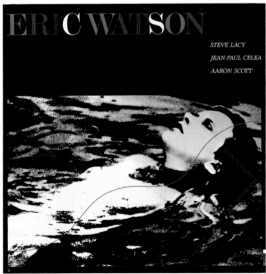

486. SONYA ROBINSON
"SONYA ROBINSON LIVE AT SPIRAL"
ART DIRECTION : TOMOHIRO ITAMI
PHOTOGRAPHY : KATSUHIRO ICHIKAWA
YEAR OF RELEASE : 1989
RECORD CO. : SPIRAL(JAPAN)
RECORD NO. : 28CD-N007

487. ERIC WATSON
"YOUR NIGHT IS MY TOMORROW"
ART DIRECTION : BERNARD AMIARD
YEAR OF RELEASE : 1987
RECORD CO. : OWL/NEC AVENUE(JAPAN)
RECORD NO. : A29C-1033

488. PUMP UP THE VOLUME
ART DIRECTION : JA
DESIGN : GEORGOPOULOS DESIGN, INC.
YEAR OF RELEASE : 1990
RECORD CO. : MCA/WEA(JAPAN)
RECORD NO. : WMC5-234

489. MELÍSA MORGAN "THE LADY IN ME"
ART DIRECTION : TOMMY STEELE
DESIGN : HEATHER VAN HAAFTEN
PHOTOGRAPHY : VICTORIA HABERSTOCK
YEAR OF RELEASE : 1990
RECORD CO. : CAPITOL/TOSHIBA EMI(JAPAN)
RECORD NO. : TOCP-6273

490.TECHNOTRONIC
"TRIP ON THIS ! THEREMIXES"
ART DIRECTION : MANHATTAN DESIGN
PHOTOGRAPHY : ELLEN CAREY
YEAR OF RELEASE : 1990
RECORD CO. : SBK

491. VARIOUS ARTISTS "JAM HARDER"
ART DIRECTION : LEN PELTIER
DESIGN : LEN PELTIER
PHOTOGRAPHY : LEN PELTIER
YEAR OF RELEASE : 1990
RECORD CO. : A & M

Front & Inside spreads

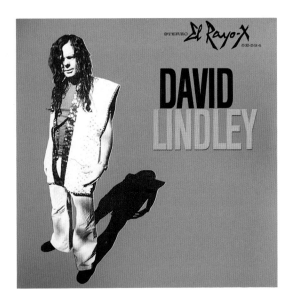

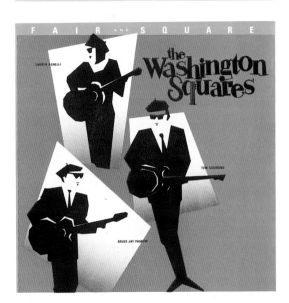

492. DAVID LINDLEY "EL RAYO-X"

ART DIRECTION : JIMMY WACHTEL

DESIGN : JIMMY WACHTEL

PHOTOGRAPHY : KAZ SAKAMOTO

RECORD CO. : ELEKTRA/WEA(JAPAN)

RECORD NO. : WPCP-3443

493. B-52'S

ART DIRECTION : SUE AB SURD

PHOTOGRAPHY : GEORGE DU BOSE

YEAR OF RELEASE : 1979

RECORD CO. : ISLAND/POLYSTAR(JAPAN)

RECORD NO. : PSCD-1056

494. THE WASINGTON SQUARES
"FAIR AND SQUARE"

DESIGN : BRYANT + ASSOCIATES

YEAR OF RELEASE : 1989

RECORD CO. : GOLD CASTLE

495. BRITISH GIRL SINGERS OF SIXTIES
"HERE COME THE GIRL"

ART DIRECTION : NEIL DELL/BIG 1

DESIGN : NEIL DELL/BIG 1

YEAR OF RELEASE : 1990

RECORD CO. : SEQUEL

496. THE BEAT ERA VOL.1
"WATCH YOUR STEP"
ART DIRECTION : NEIL DELL/BIG 1
DESIGN : NEIL DELL/BIG 1
YEAR OF RELEASE : 1990
RECORD CO. : SEQUEL

497. THE MOCK TURTLES
"MAGIC BOOMERANG TAKE YOUR TIME"
DESIGN : NAIL ON THE HEAD DESIGN
YEAR OF RELEASE : 1990
RECORD CO. : IMAGINARY

498. THE MOCK TURTLES "LAY ME DOWN"
DESIGN : NAIL ON THE HEAD DESIGN
YEAR OF RELEASE : 1990
RECORD CO. : IMAGINARY

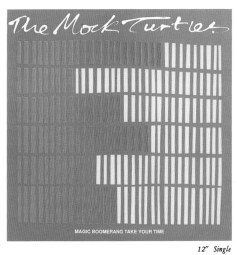

12" Single

12" Single

12" Single Back

12" Single Front

499. SHACK "I KNOW YOU WELL"
YEAR OF RELEASE : 1990
RECORD CO. : GHETIO

500. NEMOURS JN. BAPTISTE "TI CAROLE"
DESIGN : LEE-MYLES ASSOC
RECORD CO. : IBO

501. P. FUNK
"PARLIAMENT'S GREATEST HITS, UNCUTFUNK
…THE BOMB"
DESIGN : HERB POWERS, MARK WILDER
YEAR OF RELEASE : 1990
RECORD CO. : CASABLANCA/POLYSTAR(JAPAN)
RECORD NO. : PSCW-1017

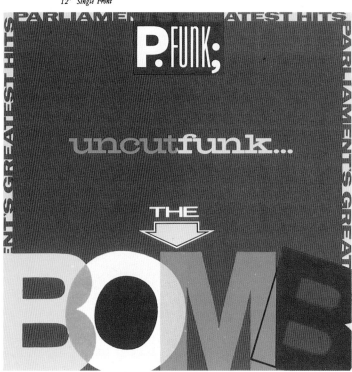

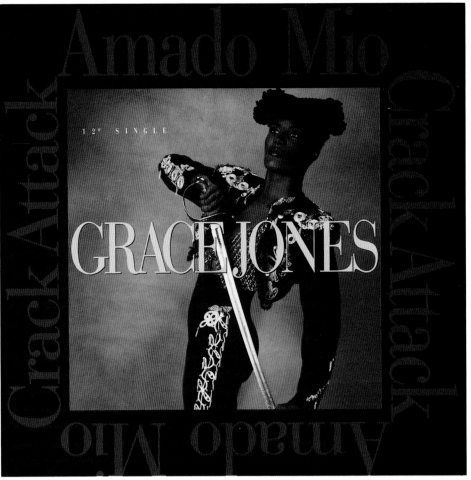

12″ Single Front

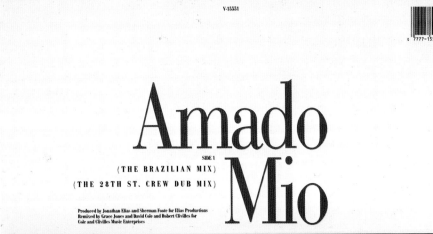

12″ Single Back

502. GRACE JONES "AMADO MIO"

ART DIRECTION : TOMMY STEELE, JEFFERY FEY

DESIGN : JEFFERY FEY

PHOTOGRAPHY : GREG GORMAN

YEAR OF RELEASE : 1990

RECORD CO. : CAPITOL

503. MICH LIVE "ONCE"

ART DIRECTION : TOMOHIRO ITAMI

YEAR OF RELEASE : 1990

RECORD CO. : SPIRAL(JAPAN)

RECORD NO. : 28CD-NO11

504. LOUIE LOUIE "THE STATE I'M IN"

ART DIRECTION : MARY MAURER

PHOTOGRAPHY : RANDEE ST. NICHOLAS

YEAR OF RELEASE : 1990

RECORD CO. : EPIC/EPIC SONY(JAPAN)

RECORD NO. : ES•CA-5156

505. YOSHIYUKI OHSAWA "SERIOUS BARBARIAN II"

ART DIRECTION : NOBUAKI TAKAHASHI

DESIGN : NOBUAKI TAKAHASHI

PHOTOGRAPHY : NAOTO OHKAWA

YEAR OF RELEASE : 1989

RECORD CO. : EPIC SONY(JAPAN)

RECORD NO. : ESCS 1001

506. THIS IS ACID JAZZ "VOLUME ONE"
DESIGN : DAVE BRUBAKER
PHOTOGRAPHY : ADAM FRIEDMAN
RECORD CO. : ACID JAZZ

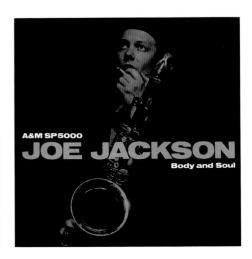

508. CHARLIE PARKER
  "THE ORIGINAL RECORDINGS OF CHARLIE PARKER"
ART DIRECTION : RICK HUNT
DESIGN : SHERYL LUTZ-BROWN
PHOTOGRAPHY : WILLIAM GOTTLIEB
YEAR OF RELEASE : 1988
RECORD CO. : POLYDOR(JAPAN)
RECORD NO. : J28J 20280

509. MARTHA HAYES
  "A HAYES NAMED MARTHA"
SUPERVISION : HERB DEXER
DESIGN : LEICHMAN-SEIDE ASSOCIATES
RECORD CO. : FRESH SOUND

510. JOE JACKSON "BODY AND SOUL"
DESIGN : QUANTUM
PHOTOGRAPHY : CHARLES REILLY
YEAR OF RELEASE : 1984
RECORD CO. : A & M/PONY CANYON(JAPAN)
RECORD NO. : D22Y-3376

507. LITTLE CREATURES
"NEED YOUR LOVE"
ART DIRECTION : NORIHIRO UEHARA
DESIGN : NORIHIRO UEHARA
PHOTOGRAPHY : HIROYUKI SHINOHARA
YEAR OF RELEASE : 1991
RECORD CO. : MIDI(JAPAN)
RECORD NO. : MDDZ-53

511. BLOSSOM DEARIE "PIANO"
PHOTOGRAPHY : J.-J. TILCHE
YEAR OF RELEASE : 1990
RECORD CO. : FRESH SOUND

512. THE CHORDETTES
DESIGN : PHILL SMEE
YEAR OF RELEASE : 1962
RECORD CO. : ACE

513. GUANA BATZ
"LONDON SHARKS HELD DOWN
TO C. D. ···AT LAST"
YEAR OF RELEASE : 1990
RECORD CO. : J.A.P. (JAPAN)
RECORD NO. : JPCP-5

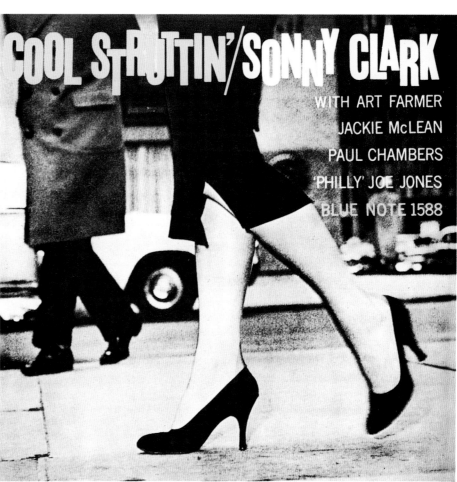

514. SONNY CLARK "COOL STRUTTIN'"
DESIGN : REID MILES
PHOTOGRAPHY : FRANCIS WLOFF
YEAR OF RELEASE : 1986
RECORD CO. : BLUE NOTE/TOSHIBA EMI(JAPAN)
RECORD NO. : CJ28-5059

515. THE FOUR TOPS "THEIR GREATEST HITS"
YEAR OF RELEASE : 1990
RECORD CO. : TELSTAR/BMG VICTOR(JAPAN)
RECORD NO. : R32M-1024

516. THE ED HIGGINS TRIO.
ART DIRECTION : ARUID CASLER
PHOTOGRAPHY : SERGE SEYMOUR
RECORD CO. : FRESH SOUND

**517. BLACK ORPHEUS,
THE ORIGINAL MOTION PICTURE
SOUNDTRACK**
DESIGN : ALTHEA LOGLIA
YEAR OF RELEASE : 1990
RECORD CO. : POLYGRAM

518. BILL EVANS TRIO "HOMEWOOD"
YEAR OF RELEASE : 1990
RECORD CO. : RED BIRD

519. VARIOUS ARTISTS "TOWNSHIP"
DESIGN : STEVE LANE, STEVE BARROW
YEAR OF RELEASE : 1990
RECORD CO. : TROJAN WORLD

520. VARIOUS ARTISTS "TRANSKEI SPECIAL"
DESIGN : STEVE LANE, STEVE BARROW
YEAR OF RELEASE : 1990
RECORD CO. : TROJAN WORLD

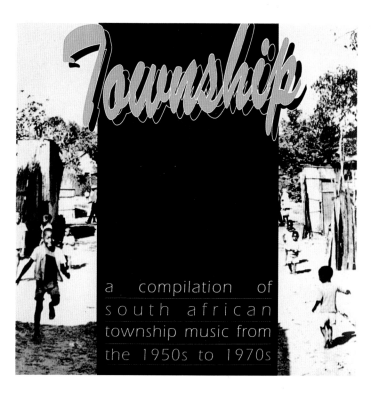

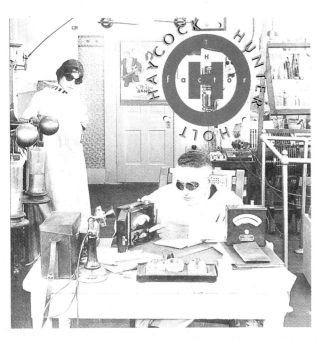

521. 5 STAR "ROCK THE WORLD"
ART DIRECTION : THE LEISURE PROCESS?
DESIGN : THE LEISURE PROCESS
YEAR OF RELEASE : 1988
RECORD CO. : BMG VICTOR(JAPAN)
RECORD NO. : R32P-1165

522. DAVE STEWART AND BARBARA GASKIN
"AS FAR AS DREAMS CAN GO"
DESIGN : STYLOROUGE
PHOTOGRAPHY : JENNY GASKIN
YEAR OF RELEASE : 1988
RECORD CO. : RYKODISC/MIDI(JAPAN)
RECORD NO. : 32MD-1035

523. THE H FACTOR "HAYCOCK・HUNTER・HOLT"
YEAR OF RELEASE : 1989
RECORD CO. : I.R.S./VICTOR(JAPAN)
RECORD NO. : VICP-18

524. JERRY HARRISON "CASUAL GODS"
DESIGN : M & CO.
PHOTOGRAPHY : M. BAYTOFF, BLACK STAR
YEAR OF RELEASE : 1990
RECORD CO. : SIRE/PHONOGRAM(JAPAN)
RECORD NO. : 32PD-449

12″ Single

525. MAUREEN
  "WHERE HAS ALL THE LOVE GONE"
DESIGN : ABRAHAMSPANTS
PHOTOGRAPHY : SLMON FOWLER
YEAR OF RELEASE : 1990
RECORD CO. : POLYDOR

526. THE DURUTTI COLUMN
  "THE GUITAR AND OTHER MACHINES"
ART DIRECTION : 8VO
DESIGN : 8VO
PHOTOGRAPHY : B/W TREVOR KEY
RECORD CO. : FACTORY/COLUMBIA(JAPAN)
RECORD NO. : 33CY-2010

527. MADONNA "LIKE A PRAYER"
ART DIRECTION : JERI HEIDEN
DESIGN : JERI HEIDEN
PHOTOGRAPHY : HERB RITTS
LOGO DESIGN : MARGO CHASE
YEAR OF RELEASE : 1989
RECORD CO. : WARNER/WARNER PIONEER(JAPAN)
RECORD NO. : 22P2-2650

533. WHISPERS "MORE OF THE NIGHT"
ART DIRECTION : TOMMY STEELE
DESIGN : CURRY DESIGN
YEAR OF RELEASE : 1990
RECORD CO. : CAPITOL/TOSHIBA EMI(JAPAN)
RECORD NO. : TOCP—6455

528. STANLEY CLARK AND GEORGE DUKE "3"
ART DIRECTION : NANCY DONALD, MARY MAURER
PHOTOGRAPHY : CHRIS CUFFARO
YEAR OF RELEASE : 1990
RECORD CO. : EPIC/EPIC SONY(JAPAN)
RECORD NO. : ES•CA-5135

529. THE SMITHEREENS "11"
ART DIRECTION : TOMMY STEELE
DESIGN : MICK HAGGERTY
PHOTOGRAPHY : DEWEY NICKS
YEAR OF RELEASE : 1989
RECORD CO. : CAPITOL/TOSHIBA-EMI(JAPAN)
RECORD NO. : TOCP-6144

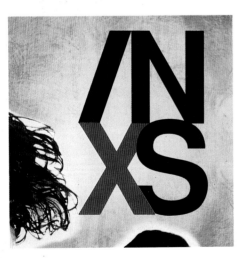

530. INXS "X"
ART DIRECTION : NICK EGAN(VIVID ID)
DESIGN : NICK EGAN AND TOM BOUMAN(VIVID ID)
PHOTOGRAPHY : MICHAEL HALSBAND
YEAR OF RELEASE : 1990
RECORD CO. : MCA/WEA(JAPAN)
RECORD NO. : WMC5-210

531. THE FIXX "INK"
ART DIRECTION : RIA LEWERKE,
FRENCHY GAUTHER
DESIGN : NORMAN MOORE
PHOTOGRAPHY : JOAN BROSSA
YEAR OF RELEASE : 1991
RECORD CO. : IMPACT
/TOSHIBA EMI(JAPAN)
RECORD NO. : TOCP-6646

532. PETER ASTOR "SUBMARINE"
PHOTOGRAPHY : RENAUD MONFOURNY
YEAR OF RELEASE : 1990
RECORD CO. : CREATION/VICTOR(JAPAN)
RECORD NO. : VICP-80

WHISPERS — MORE OF THE NIGHT

Executive Producer: Whispers for Whispers Music Inc. Production Coor

Management: Mike Gardner for the Gardner Company (213) 271-2278

Special Thanks: JIMMY BEE: Whose faith and a
over the years. You have been much more than a friend and
through our darkest hours. Tons of thanks to you. MICHAEL C
dearest friend in need and deed who has always had the
ENGEL & ENGEL: Don Engel, Jim Goodkind and the law
slayers. God bless you always. PHYLISS E. PARKER
coordinating every facet and detail needed to
relentless personal involvement and sincere w
P.S. We believe in you too! HALE MILGRIM,
your welcome of the Whispers to Capit
FOLKS: Here's a toast to a long and f
'pp' (Perfect Pitch): Heartfelt tha
know we love you. Jean Riggi
Barbara Lewis, John Fagot
was equaled only by the
release of this album.
(Nick's hair and W
Greenberg, Sta
project; best
louder th
Whisp
de

Walter Scott

Scotty Scott

Leaveil Degree

Nicholas Caldwell

Marcus Hutson

es;
es.
bert

Production
' Gregg
' Jeffries
Guitar; Zack
y, Keyboard
Harmon and

ispers. Recorded
Jeffries. Mixed at
Musicians: Drums,
r Scott. Background
: Dwayne McGhee.
ell, Chuckii Booker
y Gatling appears

by David Koenig.
udios by Craig
nd Keyboards
ers. Drum and
Arrangement.

The Dimen-
kip Saylor
ony 'A.J'
Anthony
Vocals;
ddler.

Mote
Gene
Davis
Vocal

ery Taylor. Strings, Rhythm and
 by O'Deen Mays, Jr.
management: O'Deen Mays, Jr.

EART YOUR HEART
ylor for Morning Crew Music. Recorded at Skip Saylor Recording.
Engineer: Ross Donaldson. Mixed at Skip Saylor Recording by Fil
and Keyboards: Gary Taylor. Lead Vocals: Scotty Scott. Back-
Keyboard Programming: Gary Taylor. Rhythm and String

D BLOWING
by Robert Brookins for Sac/Boy Productions. Co-Produced
Recorded at M'Bila Recording Studio and Aire LA Studios.
Engineer: Scott Weatherspoon. Mixed at Skip Saylor Record-
Synthesizer: Gordon Jones. Guitar Synthesizer Solo: Robert
and Gordon Jones. Lead Vocals: Scotty Scott. Background
Programming: Robert Brookins and Gordon Jones. Rhythm
ins and Gordon Jones. Vocal Arrangement: Robert Brookins.

GOOD TO YOU
ced by Tsuyoshi 'Taka' Takayanagi for Davis Cup Music, and
ie Recording Studio and Skip Saylor Recording. Engineered by
ay. Mixed at Aire LA Studios by Craig Burbridge Musicians:
gs, Drums, Bass and Keyboards: Tsuyoshi 'Taka' Takayanagi;
ground Vocals: Whispers. Drum Programming: Tsuyoshi 'Taka
cer. Keyboard Programming. Tsuyoshi 'Taka' Takayanagi. Rhythm
yoshi 'Taka' Takayanagi. Vocal Arrangement: Kevin Spencer; Gerald
Atlantic Recording Corporation. Kevin Spencer appears courtesy of

WHISPERS
MORE OF THE NIGHT

CDP 7 92957 2

Capitol

COMPACT DISC DIGITAL AUDIO
AAD

CAPITOL JAY 7 9

1. MORE OF THE NIGHT
2. MY HEART YOUR
HEART
3. MIND BLOWING
4. DON'T BE LATE FOR
LOVE
5. YOU ARE THE ONE
6. IS IT GOOD TO YOU
7. INNOCENT
8. GIRL DON'T MAKE
ME WAIT
9. MISUNDER-
STANDING
10. FOREVER
LOVER
11. BABES
12. I WANT 2B THE
1 4U
13. HELP THEM
SEE THE LIGHT
14. INNOCENT (Heat
of the Heat Edit)

1 Produced by Joel Davis. 2. Produced by Gary Taylor for Morning Crew Music.
3. Produced by Robert Brookins for Sac/Boy Productions. 4. Produced by
Takayanagi for Davis Cup Music and Kevin Spencer 7. Produced by
Robert Brookins for Sac/Boy Productions and Produced by Zack Harmon and
Christopher Troy for Another Production Company. 9. Produced by
sell all Tracks. 10. Produced by StarDotStar Productions.
12. Produced by Davis/Cup. 11. Produced by
McNeil. 14. Produced by Robert Brookins for Sac/Boy Productions
Producer: Whispers for Whispers Music Inc.
Inc. Manufactured by Capitol Records, Inc. Printed in U.S.A.

johnny OTIS

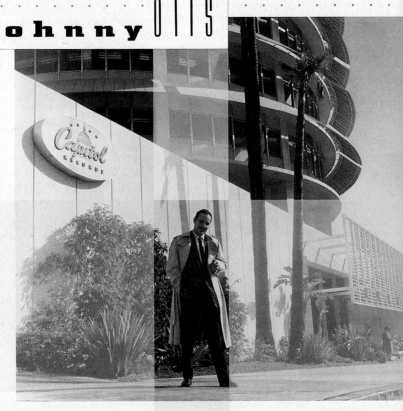

Front

. **willie and the hand jive**

Johnny Otis. Black or white? Rock and roller

. **good golly**

or big band leader? Preacher or devil's music impresario?

Sm . **crazy country hop**

Throughout his 50 years in the music busi-

. **can't you hear me callin'**

ness, Johnny Otis has always been an interesting figure. In

. **castin' my spell** (with Marie Lee)

fact (listen up Hollywood), it would make a great movie. THE

. **telephone baby**

JOHNNY OTIS STORY. A young boy of Greek-American

. **willie did the cha cha**

origin grows up among blacks in Berkeley, California and

. **livin' in misery**

learns to play drums. As a teenager, he runs off to play swing

Sm . **three girls named molly**

music with territory bands in Denver and Omaha, settles in

. **until we meet again (bye bye baby)**

World War II-era Los Angeles (just think of the cars you could

. **hum-ding-a-ling**

use for this!), marries a beautiful black woman and scores

. **baby just you**

a gig leading the house band at Club Alabam in the heart of

. **ring a ling**

L.A.'s swingin' Central Avenue scene. With only three songs

. **hey baby don't you know**

prepared, he enters a recording studio to cut his first disc. A

Sm . **let the sun shine in my life**

cigar-chomping official from the Musicians Union tells him

. **well, well, well** (with Mel Williams)

he needs one more tune or he's in violation of statute number

. **ma (he's makin' eyes at me)** (with Marie Adams) ♦

something-or-other, so Johnny ruffles through his book of

. **cold turkey** (Instrumental)

arrangements and says to his band, "'Harlem Nocturne,' boys,

. **i wonder** (with Marie Adams) ♥ ♠

and make it exotic..." *Text continued on inside of package.*

. **i'm with you** (Take 19)*

Sm . **little angel** (with Mel Williams)

. **why don't you do right? (get me some money, too)** (Instrumental) ♠ ♣

. **voodoo woman**

. **vine street swing**

Original sessions Produced by Tom Morgan

All songs Composed by Johnny Otis except ♠ Composed by E. Johnson/A. Johnson ♦ Composed by C. Conrad/S. Clare

♥ Composed by C. Gant/R. Leveen ♣ Composed by Joe McCoy *Previously Unreleased Material

Compilation Produced by Ben Vaughn. Transfer and Edit by Larry Walsh. Listening sessions engineer: Leslie Ann Jones

Sessions recorded at Capitol Studios, 1750 N. Vine Street, Hollywood and Master Recorders, 535 N. Fairfax, Los Angeles.

Ci-92858

0 7777-92858-1 5

musicians:

johnny otis—Vocals and Piano

marie adams—Vocals

mel williams—Vocals

marci lee—Vocals

ernie freeman—Piano

don johnson—Trumpet

paul lopez—Trumpet

george washington—Trombone

jack kelso—Alto, Tenor and Baritone Sax

fred harmon—Tenor and Baritone Sax

jimmy nolan—Guitar

curtis counce—Bass

earl palmer—Drums

Other unknown musicians and background vocalists contributed to these recordings but information was unavailable as of release time.

Photos courtesy of Capitol Records   Photo Archivist: Brad Benedict

Hard Jive art work courtesy of Billy Miller (KICKS Magazine)

Design: Jeffery Fey

Thanks to Dan and Fred at Bug, the Capitol Art Dept., Tom Morgan, Michael Ochs, Billy Miller, Denine, Sharon, Tina.

& Michael at Capitol and, of course, Johnny Otis.

Bug

Capitol

Back

534. JOHNNY OTIS "THE CAPITOL YEARS"
ART DIRECTION : TOMMY STEELE, JEFFERY FEY
DESIGN : JEFFERY FEY
YEAR OF RELEASE : 1989
RECORD CO. : CAPITOL

535. NUSRAT FATEH ALIKHAN AND PARTY
"SUPREME COLLECTION"
DESIGN : FUEGO-ATELIERS, FRIEDEL MUDERS
PHOTOGRAPHY : ULI BALSS ENRICO ROMERO
YEAR OF RELEASE : 1988
RECORD CO. : SERENGETI SIROCCO

536. NEW ORDER "THIEVES LIKE US"
YEAR OF RELEASE : 1984
RECORD CO. : FACTORY

12" Single

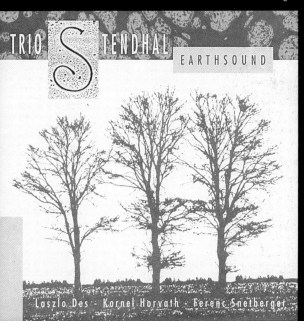

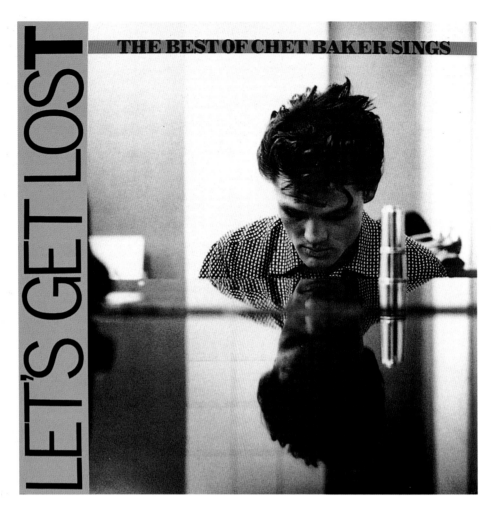

**539. CHET BAKER "LET'S GET LOST
THE BEST OF CHET BAKER SINGS"**

ART DIRECTION : RICHARD MANTEL,
FRANKO CALIGIURI
DESIGN : RICHARD MANTEL, FRANKO CALIGIURI
YEAR OF RELEASE : 1989
RECORD CO. : CAPITOL

**540. KEITH TIPPETT, ANDY SHEPPARD
"66 SHADES OF LIPSTICK"**

DESIGN : DE FACTO.
PHOTOGRAPHY : RICHARD BURBRIDE
YEAR OF RELEASE : 1990
RECORD CO. : VIRGIN

541. DONALD BYRD "BYRD JAZZ"

YEAR OF RELEASE : 1990
RECORD CO. : DELMARK/NORMA(JAPAN)
RECORD NO. : NLP5000

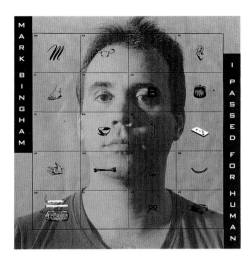

542. MARK BINGHAM "I PASSED FOR HUMAN"
DESIGN : KRISTIN JOHNSON, NEW YORK
PHOTOGRAPHY : PATTI PERRET, NEW ORLEANS
YEAR OF RELEASE : 1989
RECORD CO. : SKY RANCH

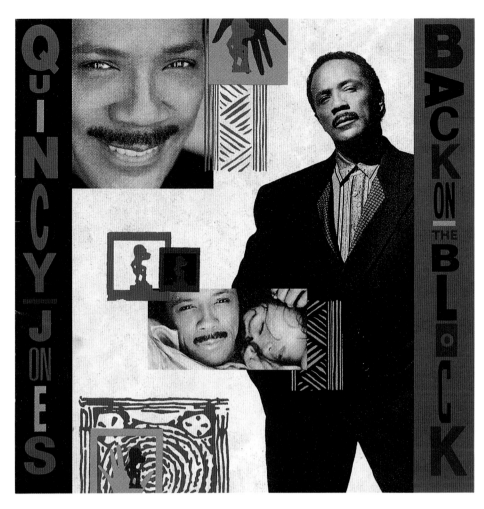

543. QUINCY JONES "BLACK ON THE BLACK"
ART DIRECTION : JERI HEIDEN
DESIGN : MARGO CHASE, ALAN DISPARTE
PHOTOGRAPHY : MATTHEW ROLSTON
YEAR OF RELEASE : 1989
RECORD CO. : WARNER/WARNER PIONEER(JAPAN)
RECORD NO. : 22P2-3118

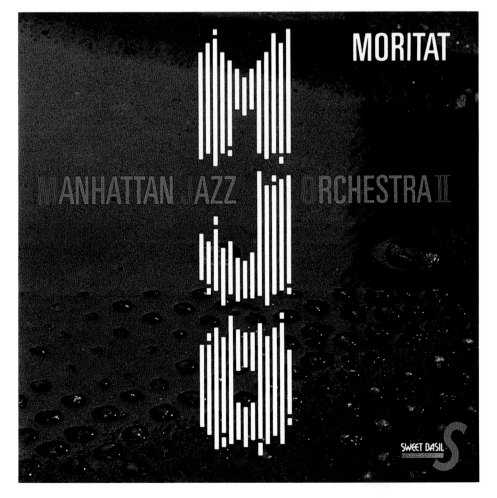

**544. MANHATTAN JAZZ ORCHESTRAII
"MORITAT"**
YEAR OF RELEASE : 1990
RECORD CO. : SWEET BASIL(JAPAN)
RECORD NO. : ALCR-72

548. TOSHINOBU KUBOTA
"SUPER DUPER VOL.2"
ART DIRECTION : RYUZOU NAGASE
DESIGN : RYUZOU NAGASE
PHOTOGRAPHY : JOJI IDE
RECORD CO. : CBS SONY(JAPAN)

545. THE JB HORNS
"PEE WEE, FRED & MACEO"
DESIGN : TAKESHI MASUDA
YEAR OF RELEASE : 1990
RECORD CO. : GRAMAVISION
/TOKUMA(JAPAN)
RECORD NO. : TKCB-30081

546. YOUNG MC
"PRINCIPAL'S OFFICE"
ART DIRECTION : SALOMON
PHOTOGRAPHY : SALOMON
YEAR OF RELEASE : 1989
RECORD CO. : DELICIOUS VINYL

12" Single

547. B.R.O.T.H.E.R.
"BEYOND THE 16TH PARALLEL"
ART DIRECTION : GATECRASH
DESIGN : TIM VARY
YEAR OF RELEASE : 1989
RECORD CO. : ISLAND

549. TOSHINOBU KUBOTA
"SUCH A FUNKY THANG!"
ART DIRECTION : YASUTAKA KATO
PHOTOGRAPHY : JOJI IDE
YEAR OF RELEASE : 1988
RECORD CO. : CBS SONY(JAPAN)
RECORD NO. : CSCL-1178

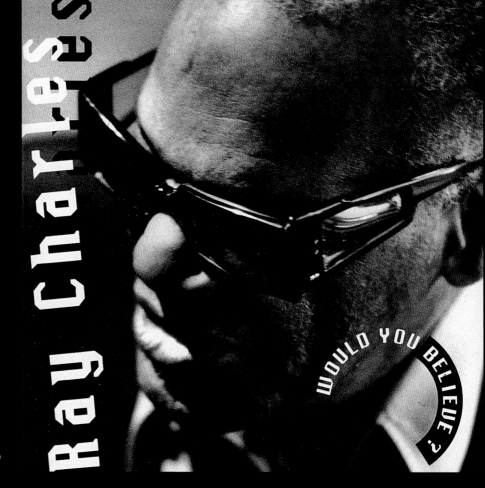

552. RAY CHARLES "WOULD YOU BELIEVE?"
ART DIRECTION : ARLETTE KOTCHOUNIAN
DESIGN : ANTOINE LEROUX-DHUYS
PHOTOGRAPHY : ARLETTE KOTCHOUNIAN
YEAR OF RELEASE : 1990
RECORD CO. : WARNER/WARNER PIONEER(JAPAN)
RECORD NO. : WPCP-4320

553. ASWAD "TOO WICKED"
PHOTOGRAPHY : ENRIQUE BADELESCU
YEAR OF RELEASE : 1990
RECORD CO. : ISLAND/POLYSTAR(JAPAN)
RECORD NO. : PSCD-1072

554. CPO "TO HELL AND BLACK"
ART DIRECTION : TOMMY STEELE
DESIGN : HEATHER VAN HAAFTEN
PHOTOGRAPHY : CAROLINE GREYSHOCK
YEAR OF RELEASE : 1990
RECORD CO. : CAPITOL

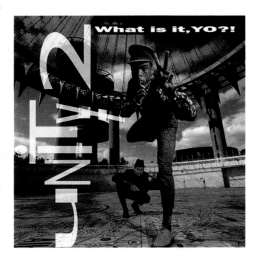

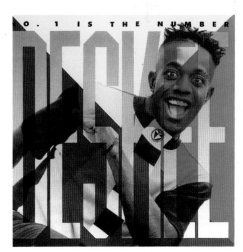

555. UNITY 2 "WHAT IS IT, YO!"
ART DIRECTION : MARY ANN DIBS, ROBIN LYNCH
DESIGN : ROBIN LYNCH
PHOTOGRAPHY : ANDY EARL
YEAR OF RELEASE : 1990
RECORD CO. : REPRISE

556. LEILAK "ROB' N' RAZ FEATURING LEILA K"
ART DIRECTION : RE-FLEX!
PHOTOGRAPHY : EWA-MARIE RUNDQUIST, EDDIE MONSOON
YEAR OF RELEASE : 1990
RECORD CO. : ARISTA/BMG VICTOR(JAPAN)
RECORD NO. : BVCA-8

557. DESKEE "NO.1 IS THE NUMBER"
ART DIRECTION : JACQUELINE MURPHY
DESIGN : JACQUELINE MURPHY
PHOTOGRAPHY : RICHARD REISS
YEAR OF RELEASE : 1990
RECORD CO. : BMG RCA

CD Single Front & Back

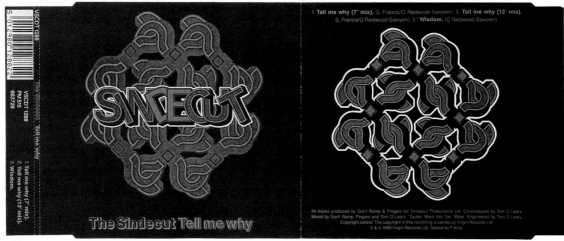

CD Single Front & Back

558. THREE TIMES DOPE
"MR. SANDMAN C.J. MACINTOSH
REMIXES"
DESIGN : CHRIS MORRIS
YEAR OF RELEASE : 1991
RECORD CO. : CITY BEAT

559. THE SINDECUT
"TELL ME WHY?"
DESIGN : FIERCE
YEAR OF RELEASE : 1990
RECORD CO. : VIRGIN

560. THE GADD GANG
"PROMOTION COPY"
ART DIRECTION : EIKO ISHIOKA
PHOTOGRAPHY : TONY BARBOZA
YEAR OF RELEASE : 1986
RECORD CO. : EPIC SONY(JAPAN)
RECORD NO. : 32•8H-87

561. LONDON BOYS "12"ERS"
RECORD CO. : WEA(JAPAN)
RECORD NO. : WMC5-51

562. QUJILA "MIX"
ART DIRECTION : NOBUAKI TAKAHASHI
DESIGN : KATUTOSHI SHIOZAKI
YEAR OF RELEASE : 1988
RECORD CO. : EPIC SONY(JAPAN)
RECORD NO. : 32•8H-5008

563. SEIKIMA II "YOUGAI"
ART DIRECTION : YASUTAKA KATO
YEAR OF RELEASE : 1990
RECORD CO. : CBS SONY(JAPAN)
RECORD NO. : CSCL-1513

564. CHAPTER 8 "FOREVER"
ART DIRECTION : TOMMY STEELE
DESIGN : ANDY ENGEL
YEAR OF RELEASE : 1988
RECORD CO. : CAPITOL

565. VARIOUS ARTISTS
"KONBIT ! BURNING RHYTHMS OF HAITI"
ART DIRECTION : JEFF GOLD, LEN PELTIER
DESIGN : LEN PELTIER, TIM STEDMAN
PHOTOGRAPHY : ELLEN PAIGE WILSON
ILLUSTRATION : SISSON BLANCHARD
YEAR OF RELEASE : 1989
RECORD CO. : A & M

566. KING SUNNY ADÉ AND HIS AFRICAN BEATS
"JUJU MUSIC"
DESIGN : BRUNO TILLEY
PHOTOGRAPHY : ADRIAN BOOT
YEAR OF RELEASE : 1982
RECORD CO. : MANGO/POLYSTAR(JAPAN)
RECORD NO. : P32D-25024

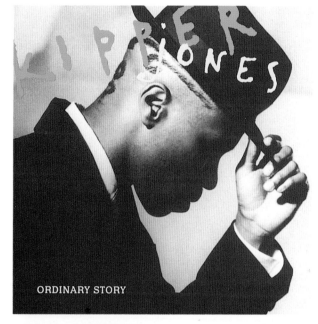

567. KIPPER JONES "ORDINARY STORY"
ART DIRECTION : MELANIE NISSEN
DESIGN : INGE SCHAAP
PHOTOGRAPHY : DAVID PROVOST
YEAR OF RELEASE : 1990
RECORD CO. : VIRGIN/VIRGIN(JAPAN)
RECORD NO. : VJCP-607

568. JIMMY CLIFF
"THINKING ABOUT THE EARTH"
ART DIRECTION : SINICHI UEDA
DESIGN : SINICHI UEDA
PHOTOGRAPHY : SWITCH MAGAGIN
YEAR OF RELEASE : 1990
RECORD CO. : SOHBI(JAPAN)
RECORD NO. : SHCP-1002

569. NINA HAGEN

YEAR OF RELEASE : 1989

RECORD CO. : MERCURY

/PHONOGRAM(JAPAN)

RECORD NO. : PPD-1088

570. SHONA LAING "SOUTH"

ART DIRECTION : RICHARD ALLAN

DESIGN : RICHARD ALLAN

PHOTOGRAPHY : KERRY BROWN

YEAR OF RELEASE : 1987

RECORD CO. : VIRGIN

571. SIOUXSIE AND THE BANSHEES "THROUGH THE LOOKING GLASS"

ART DIRECTION : CROCODILE

DESIGN : CROCODILE

PHOTOGRAPHY : EWAN FRASER

YEAR OF RELEASE : 1987

RECORD CO. : POLYDOR/POLYDOR(JAPAN)

RECORD NO. : P33P-20093

572. HI-FI SET "EYE BROW"
ART DIRECTION : WAKAKO TSUCHIYA
DESIGN : WAKAKO TSUCHIYA
PHOTOGRAPHY : MASANORI KATOH
YEAR OF RELEASE : 1988
RECORD CO. : CBS SONY(JAPAN)
RECORD NO. : 32DH-5016

**573. DAVE STEWART AND
THE SPIRITUAL COWBOYS**
DESIGN : JOHN RICHMOND
PHOTOGRAPHY : KATE GARNER
RECORD CO. : RCA/BMG VICTOR(JAPAN)
RECORD NO. : BVCP-13

574. THE MOODY BLUES "GREATEST HITS"
ART DIRECTION : MICHAEL BOYS, MARGERY GREENSPAN
DESIGN : MARGERY GREENSPAN
ILLUSTRATION : DIANA KLEIN
YEAR OF RELEASE : 1989
RECORD CO. : POLYDOR/POLYDOR(JAPAN)
RECORD NO. : P25P-20310

576. ANDREAS DORAU "DEMOKRATIE"
DESIGN : THOMAS ELSNER
PHOTOGRAPHY : KRISTIAN WAGNER
YEAR OF RELEASE : 1988
RECORD CO. : ATA TAK/WAVE(JAPAN)
RECORD NO. : EUS-2022

575. A CERTAIN RATIO "FORCE"
ART DIRECTION : ANTHONY PANAS,
A CERTAIN RATIO
DESIGN : JOHNSON PANAS
PHOTOGRAPHY : JAMES MARTIN,
DONALD JOHNSON
YEAR OF RELEASE : 1986
RECORD CO. : FACTORY/COLUMBIA(JAPAN)
RECORD NO. : 25CY-3106

577. JETHRO TULL
"SAID SHE WAS A DANCER"
DESIGN : JOHN PASCHIE
YEAR OF RELEASE : 1987
RECORD CO. : CHRYSALIS

578. LIVING IN A BOX "ROOM IN YOUR HEART"
DESIGN : WHY NOT ASSOCIATES
PHOTOGRAPHY : PAUL COX
YEAR OF RELEASE : 1989
RECORD CO. : CHRYSALIS

CD Single Front & Back

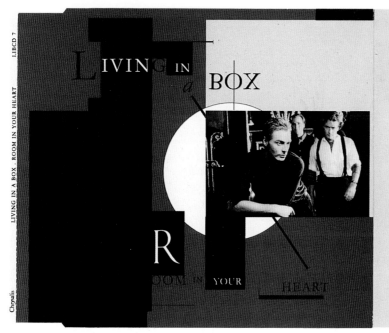

CD Single Front & Back

579. FRED FRITH "STEP ACROSS THE BORDER"
DESIGN : PETER BADER
PHOTOGRAPHY : OSCAR SALGADO
LITHOGRAPH : BUSAG, ZÜRICH
YEAR OF RELEASE : 1991
RECORD CO. : WAVE(JAPAN)
RECORD NO. : EVA-2026

580. YOHJI YAMAMOTO, YUKIHIRO TAKAHASHI "LA PENRÉE"
ART DIRECTION : KYOJI KAWAI WITH VIA BO, RINK
PHOTOGRAPHY : KENJI TOHMA
YEAR OF RELEASE : 1990
RECORD CO. : PONY CANYON(JAPAN)
RECORD NO. : PCCA-00130

Back & Front

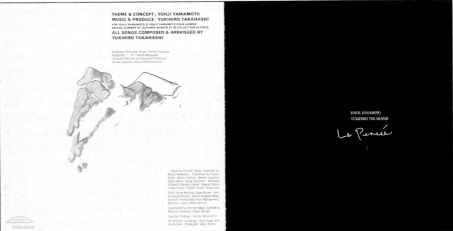

Back & Front

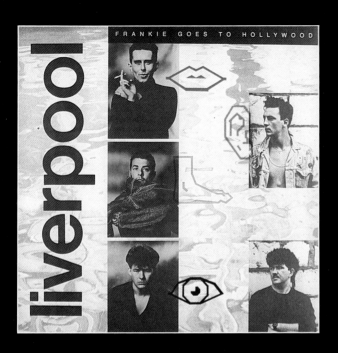

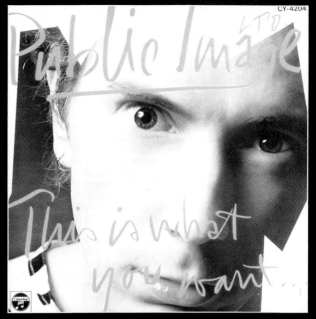

581. FRANKIE GOES TO HOLLYWOOD
  "LIVERPOOL"
DESIGN : ACCIDENT
PHOTOGRAPHY : ANTON CORBIJN
YEAR OF RELEASE : 1986
RECORD CO. : ISLAND/POLYSTAR(JAPAN)
RECORD NO. : P35D-20029

582. P I L "THIS IS WHAT YOU WANT"
YEAR OF RELEASE : 1989
RECORD CO. : VIRGIN/COLUMBIA(JAPAN)
RECORD NO. : CY-4204

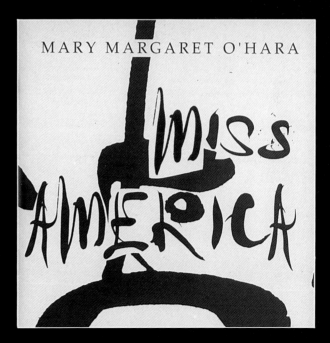

583. LE ZEMITH DE CAINSBOURG
ART DIRECTION : HUART/CHOLLEY
PHOTOGRAPHY : CLAUDE GASSIAN
YEAR OF RELEASE : 1989
RECORD CO. : PHONOGRAM

584. MARY MARGARET ÓHARA "MISS AMELICA"
ART DIRECTION : DON ROOKE, HEATHER CAMERON
DESIGN : M2 O'H
PHOTOGRAPHY : DON ROOKE, HEATHER CAMERON
YEAR OF RELEASE : 1988
RECORD CO. : VIRGIN/VIRGIN(JAPAN)
RECORD NO. : VJD-32204

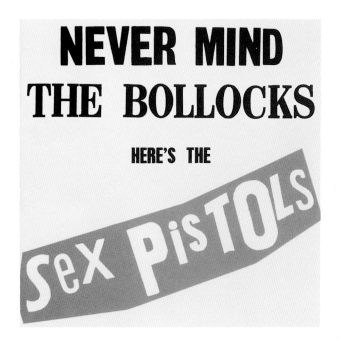

585. SEX PISTOLS
"NEVER MIND THE BOLLOCKS"
ART DIRECTION : JAMIE REID
DESIGN : JAMIE REID
ILLUSTRATION : JAMIE REID
YEAR OF RELEASE : 1977
RECORD CO. : VIRGIN/VIRGIN(JAPAN)
RECORD NO. : VJD-28093

586. THE KINKS "STATE OF CONFUSION"
DESIGN : HOWARD FRITZSON
PHOTOGRAPHY : ROBERT ELLIS
YEAR OF RELEASE : 1983
RECORD CO. : ARISTA/BMG VICTOR(JAPAN)
RECORD NO. : B20D-51006

587. SOS BAND "1980/1987···THE HIT MIXES"
YEAR OF RELEASE : 1989
RECORD CO. : TABU/CBS SONY(JAPAN)
RECORD NO. : 25DP-5377

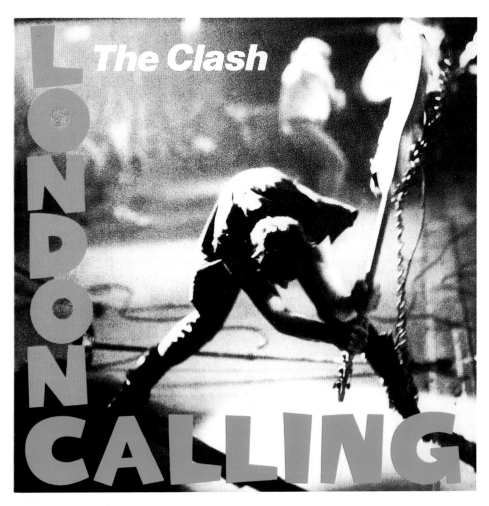

588. THE CLASH "LONDON CALLING"
DESIGN : RAY LOWRY
PHOTOGRAPHY : PENNIE SMITH
YEAR OF RELEASE : 1979
RECORD CO. : CBS/EPIC SONY(JAPAN)
RECORD NO. : 25・8P-5060

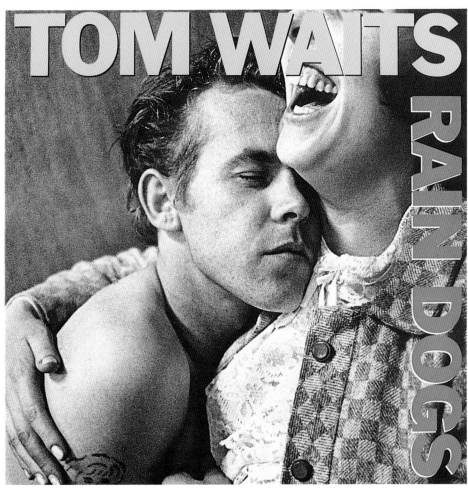

589. TOM WAITS "RAIN DOGS"
PHOTOGRAPHY : ROBERT FRANK
YEAR OF RELEASE : 1985
RECORD CO. : ISLAND/POLYSTAR(JAPAN)
RECORD NO. : R25D-2017

**590. THE BOBBY KONDERS PROJECT
"COOL CALM & COLLECTIVE"**
DESIGN : ESP
YEAR OF RELEASE : 1990
RECORD CO. : DESIRE

591. WEATHER REPORT "DOMINO THEORY"
DESIGN : LANE/DONALD
YEAR OF RELEASE : 1984
RECORD CO. : CBS/CBS SONY(JAPAN)
RECORD NO. : 35DP-140

**592. NED'S ATOMIC DUSTBIN
"UNTIL YOU FIND OUT"**
DESIGN : HELGA
YEAR OF RELEASE : 1990
RECORD CO. : CHAPTER22

593. TANANAS SPIRAL

ART DIRECTION : JUN EBIHARA

DESIGN : JUN EBIHARA

YEAR OF RELEASE : 1991

RECORD CO. : QUATTRO(JAPAN)

RECORD NO. : QTCY-1016

594. THROWING MUSES

PHOTOGRAPHY : RICHARD DONELLY

YEAR OF RELEASE : 1987

RECORD CO. : 4AD/COLUMBIA(JAPAN)

RECORD NO. : COCY-6142

595. THE BLUE HEARTS "TRAIN TRAIN"

ART DIRECTION : ITSUO SUGIURA

DESIGN : ITSUO SUGIURA

PHOTOGRAPHY : JUNICHI TAKAHASHI

ILLUSTRATION : ITSUO SUGIURA

YEAR OF RELEASE : 1988

RECORD CO. : MELDAC(JAPAN)

RECORD NO. : MED-50

596. TOKYO SKA PARADISE ORCHESTRA

ART DIRECTION : ASA-CHANG

DESIGN : YUKIO MIYAZAKI

YEAR OF RELEASE : 1990

RECORD CO. : EPIC SONY(JAPAN)

RECORD NO. : ESCB 1113

Inside spreads

597. HITOSHI UEKI "SUDARA DENSETSU"

ART DIRECTION : KAZUMA KOIDE

DESIGN : HAJIME FUJII

YEAR OF RELEASE : 1990

RECORD CO. : FUN HOUSE(JAPAN)

RECORD NO. : FHCF-1088

601. SUCHADARAPARR "BIG PROJECT OF SUCHADARA"
ART DIRECTION : HAJIME ANZAI, MASAYUKI KAWAKATSU
DESIGN : MIKI SEKINE
PHOTOGRAPHY : KENJI MIURA
YEAR OF RELEASE : 1990
RECORD CO. : FILE(JAPAN)
RECORD NO. : 23MF-020D

598. GO-BANG'S
"ROCK'N ROLL SANTACLAUS"
ART DIRECTION : JUNICHI SOMEDA
DESIGN : JUNICHI SOMEDA,
MIKA MURAI, HEAD BUTT'S
PHOTOGRAPHY : JUNICHI SOMEDA,
MAMORU MINAMIURA
YEAR OF RELEASE : 1990
RECORD CO. : PONY CANYON(JAPAN)
RECORD NO. : PCDA-00139

599. S-KEN AND HOTBOMBOMS "SEVEN ENEMIES"
ART DIRECTION : YOSHIRO KAJITANI
DESIGN : YOSHIRO KAJITANI
YEAR OF RELEASE : 1990
RECORD CO. : POLYDOR(JAPAN)
RECORD NO. : POCH-1034

600. GEORGE TOKORO & NASTY
"HEAVY LIGHT"
ART DIRECTION : KENJI ISHIKAWA
DESIGN : KENJI ISHIKAWA, YUKIO MIYAZAKI
PHOTOGRAPHY : HIDEO KAWAHARA
YEAR OF RELEASE : 1988
RECORD CO. : EPIC SONY(JAPAN)
RECORD NO. : 32・8H-5042

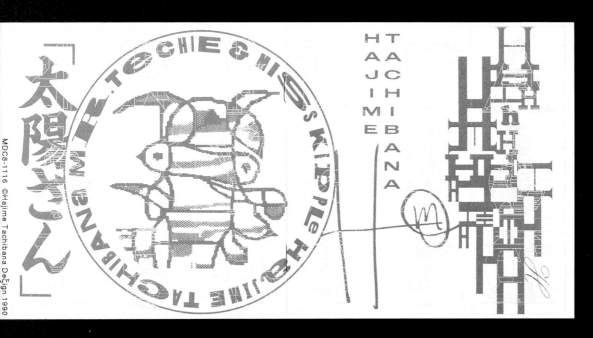

602. MALCOLM McLAREN
"WORLD FAMOUS SUPREME TEAM SHOW!!"

YEAR OF RELEASE : 1990
RECORD CO. : VIRGIN/VIRGIN(JAPAN)
RECORD NO. : VJCP-2807

603. HAJIME TACHIBANA
"HAJIME YOKEREBA SUBETEYOSHI"

DESIGN : HAJIME TACHIBANA
YEAR OF RELEASE : 1990
RECORD CO. : MIDI(JAPAN)
RECORD NO. : MDC8-1116

604. S.O.S BAND "IN ONE GO"
DESIGN : FUHE & WOLF
YEAR OF RELEASE : 1989
RECORD CO. : CBS SHCALLPLATTEN

605. GROOVE B CHILL "HIP HOP MUSIC"
ART DIRECTION : LEN PELTIER
DESIGN : F RON MILLER
ILLUSTRATION : CHRISTOPHER HILL
YEAR OF RELEASE : 1990
RECORD CO. : A & M

**606. RECKLESS SLEEPERS
"BIG BOSS SOUNDS"**
ART DIRECTION : RON SCARSELLI
DESIGN : GEOFF GANS
PHOTOGRAPHY : JAMES HAMILTON
YEAR OF RELEASE : 1988
RECORD CO. : I.R.S./VICTOR(JAPAN)
RECORD NO. : VDP-1436

12" Single

607. TAKAKO SHIRAI "BOB"
ART DIRECTION : MITSUO SHINDO
DESIGN : SATOSHI NAKAMURA
PHOTOGRAPHY : KENJI MIURA
YEAR OF RELEASE : 1990
RECORD CO. : POLYSTAR(JAPAN)
RECORD NO. : PSCR-1005

608. FLIPPER'S GUITAR
"THREE CHEERS FOR OUR SIDE"
DESIGN : SAWAKO NAKAJIMA
PHOTOGRAPHY : MITSUO SHINDO
YEAR OF RELEASE : 1989
RECORD CO. : POLYSTAR(JAPAN)
RECORD NO. : H30R-10004

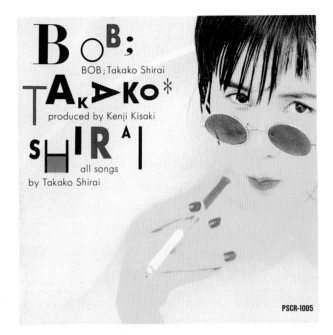

609. PIZZICATO FIVE "BELLISIMA!"
ART DIRECTION : MITSUO SHINDO
DESIGN : MITSUO SHINDO
YEAR OF RELEASE : 1988
RECORD CO. : CBS SONY(JAPAN)
RECORD NO. : 32DH-5126

610. SQUEEZE "A ROUND AND A BOUT"
DESIGN : STYLOROUGE
YEAR OF RELEASE : 1990
RECORD CO. : IRS/VICTOR(JAPAN)
RECORD NO. : VICP-44

Special PACKAGE

**611. 10 ANNIVERSAIRE CHAQUE DECENNIE
RÊVE LA SUIVANTE**
DESIGN : OLIVIER BONTEMPS,
MARK MATTOCK,
CHRISTOPHE VALDEJO POUR
YEAR OF RELEASE : 1990
RECORD CO. : VIRGIN(FRANCE)

612. D'ERLANGER "BASILISK"
DESIGN : KATZ-MIYAKE(MIYAKE-DESIGN),
SHINTARO IWASA(MIYAKE-DESIGN)
PHOTOGRAPHY : TAKASHI MATSUDA
YEAR OF RELEASE : 1990
RECORD CO. : BMG VICTOR(JAPAN)
RECORD NO. : BVCR-1

613. SOFT BALLET "3 [drai]"

ART DIRECTION : KEIICHIRO MUKAI

DESIGN : KEIICHIRO MUKAI

PHOTOGRAPHY : NAOTO SOMESE

YEAR OF RELEASE : 1990

RECORD CO. : ALFA(JAPAN)

RECORD NO. : ALCA-86

614. DE-LAX "NEUROMANCER"

ART DIRECTION : KATZ-MIYAKE

DESIGN : KATZ-MIYAKE

PHOTOGRAPHY : HITOSHI IWAKIRI

YEAR OF RELEASE : 1990

RECORD CO. : FOR LIFE(JAPAN)

RECORD NO. : FLC-4007

615. RC SUCCESSION "BABY A GO GO"
ART DIRECTION : ANDREW ELLIS(ICON, LONDON)
DESIGN : ANDREW ELLIS(ICON, LONDON)
PHOTOGRAPHY : HISAKO OHKUBO(PLUS TEN)
YEAR OF RELEASE : 1990
RECORD CO. : TOSHIBA EMI(JAPAN)
RECORD NO. : TOTT-5820

616. THE STREET SLIDERS
"NASTY CHILDREN"
ART DIRECTION : KEIJI UYEDA
(AFTER HOURS STUDIO)
DESIGN : KEIJI UYEDA(AFTER HOURS STUDIO)
HIROKO UMEZAWA
PHOTOGRAPHY : KENJI MIURA
ILLUSTRATION : GENTAROH UYEDA
YEAR OF RELEASE : 1990
RECORD CO. : EPIC SONY(JAPAN)
RECORD NO. : ESCB 1118

617. YUKIHIRO TAKAHASHI
"A DAY IN THE NEXT LIFE"
ART DIRECTION : MITUO SHINDO
DESIGN : M. SHINDO & K. FUJIKAWA,
YOSHIKI KANAZAWA
PHOTOGRAPHY : KENJI MIURA
YEAR OF RELEASE : 1991
RECORD CO. : TOSHIBA EMI(JAPAN)
RECORD NO. : TOCT-6032

CD Single & CD

618. STING "ALL THIS TIME"

YEAR OF RELEASE : 1990
RECORD CO. : A & M

619. STING "THE SOUL CAGES"

DESIGN : RICHARD FRANKEL, LEN PELTIER
PHOTOGRAPHY : GUZMAN
ILLUSTRATION : STEVEN CAMPBALL
YEAR OF RELEASE : 1991
RECORD CO. : A & M/PONY CANYON(JAPAN)
RECORD NO. : PCCY-10168

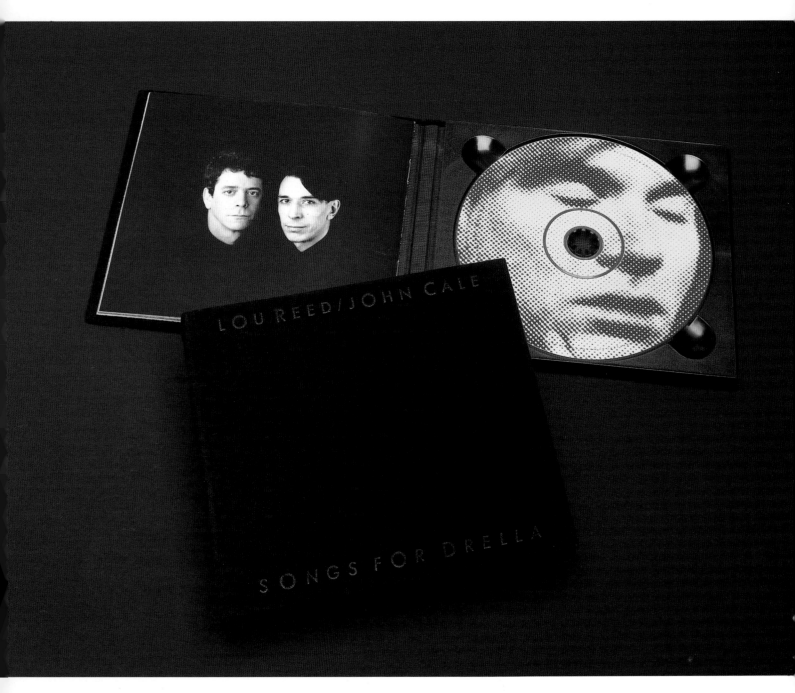

620. LOU REED, JOHN CALE "SONGS FOR DRELLA"
ART DIRECTION : SYLVIA REED, TOM RECCHION
DESIGN : SYLVIA REED, TOM RECCHION
PHOTOGRAPHY : JAMES HAMILTON, BILLY NAME
YEAR OF RELEASE : 1990
RECORD CO. : SIRE/WARNER-PIONEER(JAPAN)
RECORD NO. : WPCP-3455

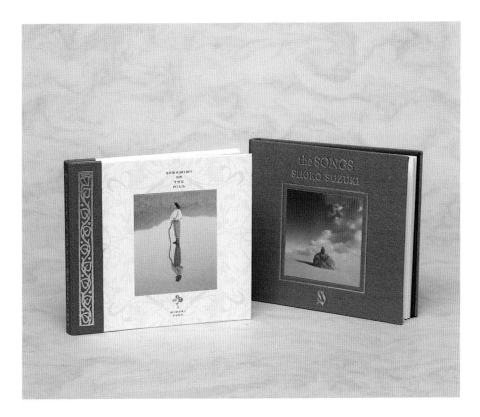

621. MIMORI YUSA
"SORAMIMI ON THE HILL"
ART DIRECTION : KENJI ISHIKAWA
DESIGN : YUKIO MIYAZAKI
PHOTOGRAPHY : GEN MURAKOSHI
YEAR OF RELEASE : 1988
RECORD CO. : EPIC SONY(JAPAN)
RECORD NO. : 35·8H-5O46

622. SHOKO SUZUKI "THE SONGS"
ART DIRECTION : KENJI ISHIKAWA(THE GARDEN)
DESIGN : FUMIKO HIRANO
PHOTOGRAPHY : YORIHITO YAMAUCHI
YEAR OF RELEASE : 1990
RECORD CO. : EPIC SONY(JAPAN)
RECORD NO. : QY·8H-90082

623. TOMOYASU HOTEI "DÉJA-VU"
ART DIRECTION : KATSU NAGAISHI
DESIGN : TOSHIAKI UESUGI
PHOTOGRAPHY : KAZUHIKO SONOKI
YEAR OF RELEASE : 1990
RECORD CO. : TOSHIBA EMI(JAPAN)
RECORD NO. : TOCT-5928

624. SHOUKICHI KINA AND CHAMPLOOSE
"NIRAIKANAI PARADISE"

ART DIRECTION : AKIRA UTUMI

DESIGN : HAJIME KOBAYASHI,
YOSHIKI KANAZAWA

PHOTOGRAPHY : JIYUNAI NAKAGAWA

YEAR OF RELEASE : 1990

RECORD CO. : TOSHIBA EMI(JAPAN)

RECORD NO. : TOCP 6270

625. THE MAGNETS "LIVE FORTRESS"

ART DIRECTION : KAZUO FUKUDA

PHOTOGRAPHY : MOMOTARO

YEAR OF RELEASE : 1990

RECORD CO. : CAPTAIN(JAPAN)

RECORD NO. : WNF-8011-CD

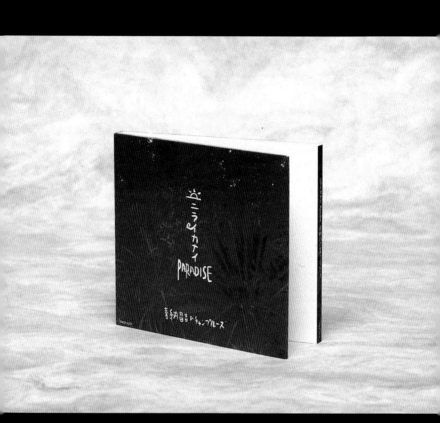

626. MADONNA "THE IMMACULATE COLLECTION"
ART DIRECTION : JERI HEIDEN
DESIGN : JERI HEIDEN, JOHN HEIDEN
PHOTOGRAPHY : HERB RITTS
RECORD CO. : SIRE/WARNER-PIONEER(JAPAN)
RECORD NO. : WPCP-4000

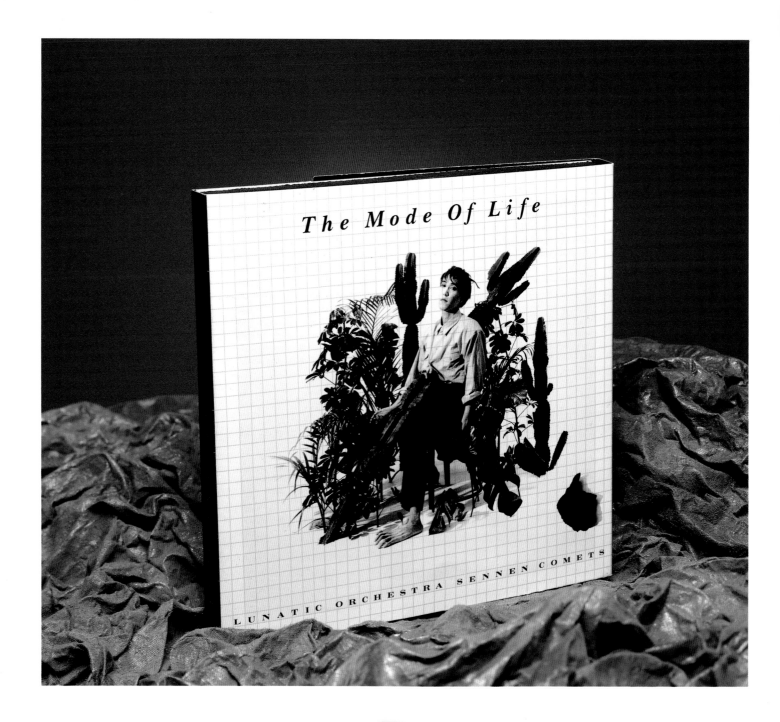

Inside spreads

627. LUNATIC ORCHESTRA(SENNEN COMETS)
"THE MODE OF LIFE"

ART DIRECTION : YASUTAKA KATO

DESIGN : YASUTAKA KATO

PHOTOGRAPHY : HARUHI FUJII

ILLUSTRATION : KEIKO HIRANO

YEAR OF RELEASE : 1990

RECORD CO. : CBS SONY(JAPAN)

RECORD NO. : CSCL 1181

628. LÄ-PPISCH "MAKE"

ART DIRECTION : MASAAKI FUKUSHI(HANDS-CREATIVE)
DESIGN : MASARU YAMACHIKA(HANDS-CREATIVE),
KENYA MORI(HANDS-CREATIVE)
PHOTOGRAPHY : YOSHIAKI SUGIYAMA
ART WORK : KENYA MORI(HANDS-CREATIVE),
YOSHIKUNI OKABE, KYRA LEE
YEAR OF RELEASE : 1990
RECORD CO. : VICTOR(JAPAN)
RECORD NO. : VICL-60

629. GO-BANG'S "THE TV SHOW"

ART DIRECTION : JUNICHI SOMEDA
DESIGN : JUNICHI SOMEDA,
KAZUO FUKUDA & HEAD BUTT'S
PHOTOGRAPHY : SOMETTI & OOR4
YEAR OF RELEASE : 1989
RECORD CO. : PONY CANYON(JAPAN)
RECORD NO. : PCCA-00003

Three dimensional effect box cover

See-Through insert with color portrait CD

630. BAUHAUS "THE SINGLES 1981-1983"
ART DIRECTION : STIFF WEAPON
DESIGN : STIFF WEAPON
PHOTOGRAPHY : FIN COSTELLO
ILLUSTRATION : STIFF WEAPON
YEAR OF RELEASE : 1989
RECORD CO. : BEGGARS BANQUET

Photo overlay with Kaleidoscope effect

631. FAIR CHILD "SEKAI NO UTA"
ART DIRECTION : KATZ-MIYAKE
DESIGN : MIYAKE DESIGN OFFICE
(SHINTARO IWASA＋KEISUKE YAGI)
PHOTOGRAPHY : MASANORI KATO
YEAR OF RELEASE : 1990
RECORD CO. : PONY CANYON(JAPAN)
RECORD NO. : PCCA-00154

632. HEART "BRIGADE"
ART DIRECTION : NORMAN MOORE
DESIGN : NORMAN MOORE
YEAR OF RELEASE : 1990
RECORD CO. : CAPITOL/TOSHIBA EMI(JAPAN)
RECORD NO. : TOCP-6129

633. 38 SPECIAL "**STRENGTH IN NUMBERS**"
ART DIRECTION : NORMAN MOORE
DESIGN : NORMAN MOORE
YEAR OF RELEASE : 1986
RECORD CO. : A & M/PONY CANYON(JAPAN)
RECORD NO. : D32Y-3012

634. PHIL COLLINS "**TWO HEARTS**"
DESIGN : PROKTOR AND STOREY
YEAR OF RELEASE : 1988
RECORD CO. : VIRGIN

635. XTC "**KING FOR A DAY**"
DESIGN : AXIS PRODUCTIONS
YEAR OF RELEASE : 1989
RECORD CO. : VIRGIN

636. THE GO-BETWEENS
"**STREETS OF YOUR TOWN**"
YEAR OF RELEASE : 1989
RECORD CO. : BEGGARS BANQUET

637. DAVID SYLVIAN "WEATHER BOX"

ART DIRECTION : RUSSELL MILLS, DAVE COPPENHALL(MC2)

DESIGN : RUSSELL MILLS, DAVE COPPENHALL(MC2)

PHOTOGRAPHY : DAVID BUCKLAND

YEAR· OF RELEASE : 1989

RECORD CO. : VIRGIN/VIRGIN(JAPAN)

RECORD NO. : VJD-251〜5

iNDeX

PHOTOGRAPHY

RECORD COMPANIES

JAPAN

ALFA RECORDS	3-5-39, Shibaura, Minato-ku, Tokyo 108 TEL: 03-3455-1791
AMERICANA RECORDS	5-3-11, Naka-Kasai, Edogawa-ku, Tokyo 134 TEL: 03-3878-6041
AVEX DD	2-7-4, Haramachida, Machida-shi, Tokyo 194 TEL: 0427-28-8664
BANDAI	1-26-6, Shinjuku, Shinjuku-ku, Tokyo 160 TEL: 03-5828-3021
BMG VICTOR	1-7-8, Shibuya, Shibuya-ku, Tokyo 150 TEL: 03-3797-9020
CAPTAIN RECORDS	5-5-5, Kojimachi, Chiyoda-ku, Tokyo TEL: 03-3239-2770
CENTURY RECORDS	3-14-12, Roppongi, Minato-ku, Tokyo 106 TEL: 03-3401-7141
COLUMBIA RECORDS	4-14-14, Akasaka, Minato-ku, Tokyo 107-11 TEL: 03-3584-8111
CROWN RECORDS	2-10-8, Akasaka, Minato-ku, Tokyo 107 TEL: 03-3582-4743
D.I.W	2-13-1, Iidabashi, Chiyoda-ku, Tokyo 102 TEL: 03-3234-5513
EDOYA RECORDS	#501, 1-4-6, Shimo-Meguro, Meguro-ku, Tokyo 153 TEL: 03-3779-2355
EPIC/SONY RECORDS	3F, 2-14-5, Akasaka, Minato-ku, Tokyo 107 TEL: 03-5563-8000
EXPLOSION WORKS	#3-212, 16-1, Tsukiji-cho, Shinjuku-ku, Tokyo 162 TEL: 03-3235-0315
FILE	8F, 1-8-18, Ebisu, Shibuya-ku, Tokyo 150 TEL: 03-3473-7941
FOR LIFE	10F, 7-8-1, Minami-Aoyama, Minato-ku, Tokyo 107 TEL: 03-3406-6951
FUN HOUSE	1-9-1, Shinjuku, Shinjuku-ku, Tokyo 160 TEL: 03-3350-8610
HUMMING BIRD	2F, 8-5-30, Akasaka, Minato-ku, Tokyo 107 TEL: 03-3479-8371
INNER DIRECTS	#202, 2-14-21, Minami-Aoyama, Minato-ku, Tokyo 107 TEL: 03-3408-9141
J.A.P	1-8-3, Hatsudai, Shibuya-ku, Tokyo 151 TEL: 03-5371-8334
JIMCO RECORDS	4-7-7, Kachidoki, Chuo-ku, Tokyo 104 TEL: 03-3534-8785
KING RECORDS	2-2-2, Otowa, Bunkyo-ku, Tokyo 112 TEL: 03-3945-2111
KITTY RECORDS	1-8-4, Ohashi, Meguro-ku, Tokyo 153 TEL: 03-3780-8611
LOB	1-20-2, Honcho, Shibuya-ku, Tokyo 151 TEL: 03-3374-6691
MCA VICTOR	2-21-7, Jingumae, Shibuya-ku, Tokyo 150 TEL: 03-3796-3811
MELDAC	6F, 1-1-1, Minami-Aoyama, Minato-ku, Tokyo 107 TEL: 03-3423-2525
MIDI	5-11-18, Minami-Aoyama, Minato-ku, Tokyo 107 TEL: 03-3498-9555
MMG	6F, 1-1-8, Shinjuku, Shinjuku-ku, Tokyo 160 TEL: 03-3225-7271
MSI	#503, 2-10, Kitazawa, Setagaya-ku, Tokyo 155 TEL: 03-3460-2721
NEC AVENUE	2-14-2, Kojimachi, Chiyoda-ku, Tokyo 102 TEL: 03-3265-6111
NIPPON PHONOGRAM	4-8-5, Roppongi, Minato-ku, Tokyo 106 TEL: 03-3479-3716
P-VINE	4-18-6, Jingumae, Shibuya-ku, Tokyo 150 TEL: 03-3408-8343
POLYDOR	1-8-4, Ohashi, Meguro-ku, Tokyo 153 TEL: 03-3780-8591
POLYSTAR	5-1-2, Minami-Aoyama, Minato-ku, Tokyo 107 TEL: 03-3406-8161
PONY CANYON	3-3-5, Kudan-Kita, Chiyoda-ku, Tokyo 102 TEL: 03-3221-3131
PUZZLIN	13-2, Rokuban-cho, Chiyoda-ku, Tokyo 102 TEL: 03-3288-5642
QUATTRO(PARCO)	15-1, Udagawa-cho, Shibuya-ku, Tokyo 150 TEL: 03-3770-4666
SFC MUSIC PUBLISHER(SOLID)	3F, 2-32-2, Sendagaya, Shibuya-ku, Tokyo 151 TEL: 03-3408-5371
SOHBI	2-10, Kojimachi, Chiyoda-ku, Tokyo 102 TEL: 03-3238-0316
SONY RECORDS	1-4, Ichigaya-Tamachi, Shinjuku-ku, Tokyo 162 TEL: 03-3266-5995
SPIRAL	5-6-23, Minami-Aoyama, Minato-ku, Tokyo 107 TEL: 03-3498-1171
TEICHIKU RECORDS	NK Bldg.Toranomon, Minato-ku, Tokyo 105 TEL: 03-3506-8700
TOKUMA JAPAN	1-18-21 Shinbashi, Minato-ku, Tokyo 105 TEL: 03-3508-4911
TOSHIBA-EMI	2-2-17, Akasaka, Minato-ku, Tokyo 107 TEL: 03-3587-9111
TRANSISTOR RECORD	2F, 1-34-1, Ookayama, Meguro-ku, Tokyo 152 TEL: 03-5701-3911
VAP	1F, 12-6, Goban-cho, Chiyoda-ku, Tokyo 102 TEL: 03-3234-5710
VICTOR MUSICAL INDUSTRIES	4-26-18, Jingumae, Shibuya-ku, Tokyo 150 TEL: 03-3746-5550
VINYL JAPAN	2F, 7-4-9, Nishi-Shinjuku, Shinjuku-ku, Tokyo
VIRGIN JAPAN	5-18-20, Sendagaya, Shibuya-ku, Tokyo 151 TEL: 03-3356-3926
VIVID SOUND	2-23-8, Shimo-Meguro, Meguro-ku, Tokyo 153 TEL: 03-3490-1070
WARNER PIONEER	1-1-1, Minami-Aoyama, Minato-ku, Tokyo 107 TEL: 03-3475-2111
WAVE	6-2-27, Roppongi, Minato-ku, Tokyo 106 TEL: 03-3408-0111
WEA MUSIC	3F, 3-8, Sanban-cho, Chiyoda-ku, Tokyo 102 TEL: 03-3221-8555

OVERSEAS

4AD RECORDS	17/19 Alma Road, London SW18 ,England TEL: 081-870-9724
A&M RECORDS	1416 North La Brea Avenue, Los Angeles, CA 90028 ,USA TEL: 213-469-2411
ACE RECORDS	48-50 Steele Road, London NW10 7AS ,England TEL: 081-453-1311
ACID JAZZ RECORDS	222 West 14th Street, New York, NY 10011 ,USA TEL: 212-727-1360
ALA BIANCA S. R. L.	Modena(Italy) 34-36, Via G. Mazzoni ,Italy TEL: 059-223897
ALLIGATOR RECORDS	P. O. Box 60234, Chicago, IL 60660 ,USA TEL: 312-973-7736
ARISTA RECORDS	6 West 57th Street, New York, NY 10019 ,USA TEL: 212-489-7400
ATLANTC	75 Rockefeller Plaza, New York, NY 10019 ,USA TEL: 212-484-6000
ATTACK RECORDS	Twyman House 31-39, Camden Road, London NW1 9LF ,England TEL: 071-267-6899
BARCLAY	89 Bvd Auguste Blanqui, 75013, Paris ,France TEL: 1-4581-1185
BBC ENTERPRISES	Wood lands, 80 Wood Lane, London W12 OTT ,England
BEAR FAMILY RECORDS	P. O. Box 1154, 2864 Vollersode ,Germany TEL: 04794-1399
BEGGARS BANQUET RECORDS	17-19 Alma Road, London SW18 1AA ,England TEL: 081-870-9912
BLUE MOON RECORDS	P. O. Box 25066, Nashville, TN 37202 ,USA TEL: 615-269-0593
BLUE NOTE	1750 N. Vine Street, Los Angeles, CA 90028 ,USA
BMG ENTERPRISES	Cavendish House, 423 New Kings Road, London SW6 4RN ,England TEL: 071-973-0011
BUDA MUSIQUE	188, Boulevard Voltaire, Paris ,France TEL: 1-40-24-01-0
CAPITOL RECORDS	1750 North Vine Street, Hollywood, CA 90028-5274 ,USA TEL: 213-871-5156
CHAMPION RECORDS	181 High Street, Harlesden, London NW10 4TE ,England TEL: 081-961-5202
CHARISMA RECORDS	1790 Broadway, New York, NY 10019 ,USA TEL: 212-586-7700

R E C O R D   C O M P A N I E S

CHRYSALIS RECORDS	645 Madison Avenue, New York, NY 10022 ,USA TEL: 212-758-3555
CITY BEAT RECORDS	17-19 Alma Road, Wandsworth, London SW18 1AA ,England TEL: 081-870-7511
CLAY RECORDS	26 Hope Street, Hanley, Stoke-on-trent ST 15BS ,England TEL: 782-273-324
COCTEAU RECORDS	3355 W. El Segundo Blvd, Hawthorne, CA 90250 ,USA TEL: 213-973-8282
CREATION RECORDS	8 Westgate Street, London E8 3RN ,England TEL: 081-986-7196
CTI RECORDS	810 Seventh Avenue, New York, NY 10019 ,USA
DELICIOUS VINYL	7471 Melrose #25, Los Angeles, CA 90046 ,USA TEL: 213-465-2700
ECM	810 Seventh Avenue, New York, NY 10019 ,USA TEL: 212-333-8100
ELEKTRA/ASYLUM/NONESUCH RECORDS	75 Rockefeller Plaza, New York,NY 10019 ,USA TEL: 212-484-7200
EMI	20 Manchester Square, London W1A 1ES ,England TEL: 071-486-4488
EMARCY	810 Seventh Avenue, New York, NY 10019 ,USA
ENIGMA ENTERTAINMENT	Calver City, CA 90231-3628 ,USA TEL: 818-587-4044
ENSIGN	645 Madison Avenue, New York, NY 10022 ,USA TEL: 212-758-3555
FACTORY COMMUNICATIONS	Charles Street, Manchester M1 7EB ,England TEL: 061-953-0251
FFRR	1 Sussex Place, London W6 9XS ,England TEL: 081-846-8090
FIRE RECORDS	P. O. Box 800, Rockville Centre, NY 11571-0800 ,USA TEL: 516-764-6200
GEFFEN RECORDS	9130 Sunset Blvd., Los Angeles, CA 90069 ,USA TEL: 213-278-9010
GOLD CASTLE	3575 Cahuenga Blvd. W. #470, Los Angeles, CA 90068 ,USA
GRAMAVISION	260 West Broadway, New York, NY 10013 ,USA TEL: 212-226-7057
GREENSLEEVES RECORDS	Unit 7, Goldhawk Industrial Estate, Brackenbury Road, London W6 0BA ,England TEL: 081-749-3277
I. R. S RECORDS	3939 Lankershim Blvd. Universal City, CA 91604 ,USA TEL: 818-508-3130
IMAGINARY ENTERTAINMENT	332 N. Dean Rd. Ave., Auburn. AL 36830 TEL: 205-821-5277
ISLAND RECORDS	14 East Fourth Street, New York, NY ,USA TEL: 212-477-8000
JARO/FUEGO	Alexanderstr. 9A D-2800, Bremen 1 TEL: 0421-78080
KAZ PRT DISTRBUTION	105 Bound Road, Mitcham, Surrey CR4 3UT ,England
KITCHENWARE RECORDS	Saint Thomas Street Stables, Newcastle upon Tyne NE1 4LE TEL: 091-232-4895
LINE RECORDS	P. O. Box 605220, D-2000 Hamburg, 60 ,Germany
LONDON RECORDS	P. O. Box 1422, Chanbllors House, Chancbllors Road, Hammersmith, London W6 9SG ,England TEL: 081-741-1234
LUKE RECORDS	8400 North East 2nd Avenue, Miami, FL 33138 ,USA TEL: 305-757-1969
MANY RECORDS	Via Fantoli, 9-20138, Milano ,Italy TEL: 02-5801-0840
MCA/SPECIAL MARKETS & PRODUCTS	70 Universal City Plaza, Universal City, CA 91608 ,USA TEL: 818-777-4090
MERCURY	810 Seventh Avenue, New York, NY 10019 ,USA TEL: 212-333-8000
MUTE RECORDS	429 Harrow Road, London W10 4RE ,England TEL: 081-969-8866
NATIVE RECORDS	P. O. Box 49, Sheffield S1 1JD ,England TEL: 0302-370889
ONE LITTLE INDIAN	3 Fransfield Grove, London E82EB ,England TEL: 254-6543
OWL RECORDS	15 Place, Saint Martin-14000, Caen ,France
PAISLEY PARK	75 Rockefeller Plaza, New York, NY 10019 ,USA
PHONOGRAM	1 Sussex Place, London W6 9XS ,England TEL: 081-846-8090
PLAY IT AGAIN SAM RECORDS	Rue De Veeweyde 90, 1070 Brussels ,Belgium TEL: 02-5144007
POLYDOR	1 Sussex Place, London W6 9XS ,England TEL: 081-846-8090
POPLLAMA PRODUCTS	P. O. Box 95364, Seattle, WA 98145-2364 ,USA TEL: 206-527-8816
PRIORITY RECORDS	6430 Sunset Blvd., Hollywood, CA 90028 ,USA TEL: 213-467-0151
PRIVATE MUSIC	9014 Melrose Avenue, Los Angeles, CA 90069 ,USA TEL: 213-859-9200
PROFILE RECORDS	740 Broadway, 7th Fl., New York, NY 10003 ,USA TEL: 212-529-2600
QWEST RECORDS	3300 Warner Blvd., Burbank, CA 91510 ,USA TEL: 818-953-3472
RCA RECORDS	1 Bedford Avenue, London WC1B 3DT ,England TEL: 1-636-8311
RELATIVITY RECORDS	149-03 R Brew Blvd., Jamaica, 11434 ,Jamaica TEL: 718-995-9200
REPRISE	75 Rockefeller Plaza, New York, NY 10019 ,USA TEL: 818-846-9090
RHYTHM KING RECORDS	Lawford House, 429 Harrow Road, London W10 4RE ,England TEL: 081-969-8866
RODGERS & COMTITI RECORDS	Via G. Frua, 7, 20146 Milano ,Italy TEL: 39-2-463705
ROUGH TRADE RECORDS	61 Collier Street, London N1 9BE ,England TEL: 071-837-6747
ROUNDER RECORDS	1 Camp Street, Cambridge, Massachusetts, 02140 ,USA TEL: 617-354-0700
RUMOUR RECORDS	Tempo House, 15 Falcon Road, London SW11 2P1 ,England TEL: 071-228-6821
RYKODISK EUROPE (HANNIBAL)	P. O. Box 2401, London W2 5SF ,England TEL: 071-727-7480
RYKODISK USA	Daniel Bldg-6th Floor, 20-22 North Third Street, Philadelphia, PA 19106 ,USA TEL: 215-629-0030
S. S. T.	USA TEL: 213-430-7687
SBK RECORDS	1290 Avenue of the Americas, New York, NY 10104 ,USA TEL: 212-492-1200
SEQUEL RECORDS	West Heath Studios, West Heath Yard, 174 Mill Lane, London NW6 1TB ,England TEL: 071-433-1641
SIRE RECORDS	75 Rockefeller Plaza, New York, NY 10019 ,USA TEL: 212-484-6830
SONY MUSIC AUSTRALIA	11-19 Hargrave Street, East Sydney, NSW 2010 ,Australia TEL: 61-2-339-025
SONY MUSIC INTERNATIONAL	51 West, 52 Street, New York, NY 10019-6165 ,USA TEL: 212-445-6399
SONY MUSIC UK	17/19 Soho Square, London W1V 6HE ,England TEL: 071-734-8181
TAMOKI-WAMBESI RECORDS	58, Picton Road, Wavertree, Liverpool L15 4LH ,England TEL: 051-734-2268
TEL: STAR RECORDS	The Studio, King Edward Mews, London SW13 9HP ,England TEL: 081-846-9946
TENOR VOSSA RECORDS	1 Coliville Place, London W1P 1HN ,England TEL: 071-636-6465
THIRD MIND RECORDS	P. O. Box 160, Canterbury, Kent CT2 TXL ,England TEL: 227-68573
TRIPLE EARTH RECORDS	1-8 WhitField Place, London W1N 9HF ,England TEL: 378-76461
TROJAN RECORDS	Twyman House 31-39, Camden Road, London NW1 9LF ,England TEL: 071-267-6899
VIRGIN RECORDS	Kensal House 553-579 Harrow Road, London W10 4RH ,England TEL: 081-968-6688
VOICE PRINT	P. O. Box 1431, London N8 7BZ ,England TEL: 081-889-0616
WARNER BROS RECORDS	3300 Warner Blvd. Burbank, CA 91505-4694 ,USA TEL: 818-953-3364
WARNER MUSIC UK	28 Kensington Church Street, London W8 4EP ,England TEL: 071-937-8844
WEA RECORDS	Electric Lightning Sta., 46, Kensington Court, London W8 5DP ,England TEL: 071-937-8844
WORKERS PLAYTIME	611 Broadway, New York, NY 10012 ,USA
ZEIDA	11 A 40, Medellin, Antioquia, Carrera 43 A N, ,Colombia TEL: 574-266-0762
ZTT RECORDS	The Blue Bldg 42-46, St. Luke's Mews, London W11 1DS ,England TEL: 071-221-5101

STAFF

ART DIRECTOR
Kimiko Ishiwatari

DESIGNERS
Kimiko Ishiwatari
Shinji Ikenoue

EDITORS
Makoto Numata
Shuichi Tokushima

PHOTOGRAPHER
Minoru Takayama

ACKNOWLEDGMENT
Roland Gebhardt
(Roland Gebhardt Design, New York)
Sarah Phillips (London)

PROJECT MANAGER
Satoshi Sugo

PUBLISHER
Shingo Miyoshi

1994年7月14日 第2刷発行

発行人　　三芳 伸吾

発行所　　ピエ・ブックス
　　　　　〒170 東京都豊島区駒込4-14-6 ビラフェニックス407
　　　　　TEL 03-3949-5010 FAX 03-3949-5650

製　版　　(株)ササキ写真製版
　　　　　〒162 東京都新宿区赤城下町25
　　　　　TEL 03-3268-8475 FAX 03-3235-5053

印刷・製本　(株)サンニチ印刷
　　　　　〒151東京都渋谷区代々木2-10-8
　　　　　TEL03-3374-6241 FAX03-3374-6252

写　植　　オフィスアスク
　　　　　〒176 東京都練馬区豊玉北5-18-13 大鳥ビル303
　　　　　TEL 03-3993-3157 FAX 03-3993-3158

ISBN4-938586-55-X C0073